THE WORK OF JESUS

The
Work of Jesus

F. F. BRUCE

KINGSWAY PUBLICATIONS
EASTBOURNE

ISBN 0 86065 300 5

Printed in Great Britain for
KINGSWAY PUBLICATIONS LTD
Lottbridge Drove, Eastbourne, E.Sussex BN23 6NT by
Richard Clay (The Chaucer Press) Ltd, Bungay, Suffolk.

TO MARGARET

CONTENTS

Preface

Introduction   11

1   'MY FATHER'S BUSINESS'   13
   'You are my Son'   13
   The descent of the dove   15
   Testing in the wilderness   16
   The good news of the kingdom   18
   A question and its answer   19
   Works of mercy and power   21
   'You are the Messiah'   24

2   THE WAY OF THE CROSS   27
   Conflict with the religious authorities   27
   Conflict with Herod Antipas   29
   Conflict in Jerusalem   30
   The question of taxation   33
   The last supper   35
   Arrest, trial and crucifixion   37

3   THE WORK GOES ON   42
   Christ risen and active   42
   The shared ministry   44
   The baptism of the Spirit   45
   The powerful name   46
   A continuing story   49

4 CHRIST OUR RIGHTEOUSNESS 51
'What the law could not do' 51
Paul's gospel 55
Getting right with God 58

5 CHRIST THE CONQUEROR 62
The powers of evil 62
The reigning Christ 64
The rout of demonic forces 65
His people's present helper 68

6 PRIEST AND SACRIFICE 71
Our great high priest 71
A sacrifice for sin 74
The finality of the gospel 77
The Christian's experience 82
The guardian of mankind 84
The pioneer of faith 85
Christ's reappearance 86

7 WORTHY IS THE LAMB 87
A book of pictures 87
Creation and redemption 88
Two points of view 90
The final triumph 91

8 BEFORE THE INCARNATION 94
Christ in creation 94
Christ with Israel in the wilderness 99

9 THE WITNESS OF PROPHECY 103
The church's earliest Bible 103
Jesus and the Son of Man 105
Son of Man and Servant of the Lord 106
'The chastisement that made us whole' 107
The Servant's witnesses 110
The righteous sufferer 112

10 THE FUTURE WORK OF CHRIST:
ACCORDING TO JOHN 114
Two 'greater works' 114
The work of judgement 115

The raising of the dead 116
Eternal life now 117
Present self-judgement 118
Response to the truth 119

11 THE FUTURE WORK OF CHRIST:
ACCORDING TO PAUL 121
First fruits and harvest 121
Resurrection and judgement 122
Resurrection life now 124
After death, what? 125
A wider perspective 126

12 THE SAVING WORK OF CHRIST 129
Unity in diversity 129
Christ our salvation 129
The means of salvation 131
Advocacy and expiation 132
The cure of sin 135
Salvation in three tenses 136
The new world 138

Index 141

Further Reading 145

PREFACE

When I was invited to write a book on *The Work of Jesus* for the Kingsway Bible Teaching Series, I accepted the invitation with certain misgivings about my ability to write in a way suitable for the purpose of the series. But misgivings of this sort should not be treated as an excuse for turning down such an invitation, but rather as a challenge to accept it and produce the kind of work desired. The result of my acceptance of the invitation now lies before the reader.

I should like to express my gratitude to the Rev. Gilbert W. Kirby, general editor of the series, for inviting me to contribute to it, and to Dr Jack Hywel-Davies, chairman of Kingsway Publications, for his encouragement. And a quite special word of gratitude must go to Miss Margaret Hogg, who as my secretary for fifteen years has co-operated in the production of many of my books. Since this is the last book for which I can rely on her help, it is fitting that it should be dedicated to her to record my appreciation of all that she has done for me.

F. F. BRUCE

INTRODUCTION

We sometimes hear preachers and lecturers on Christian doctrine talk about 'the work of Jesus' or, more fully, 'the person and work of Jesus'. A study of the person of Jesus Christ undertakes to answer the question, 'Who is he?' A study of his work undertakes to answer the question, 'What did he do?' – or rather the three questions: 'What did he do?' – 'What is he doing?' – 'What is he going to do?'.

The Bible bears witness to Jesus from a variety of viewpoints. It bears witness to him, for example, as a historical character, who lived and died between 1900 and 2000 years ago. The New Testament opens with the four gospels, which tell of his life and work in Palestine. If that is the kind of information we are looking for when we ask 'What did he do?' then the gospels will provide the answer. Some of the other New Testament writings refer back to his work on earth, and they too help to provide us with an answer along the same lines.

But the New Testament writings also bear witness to him as the one who rose from the dead and lives for evermore. We can thus ask about him in a way that we should not naturally ask about any other historical character, 'What is he doing now?' and 'What is he going to do?'. Not only so; the fact that he is risen and alive gives fuller meaning to the question 'What did he do?'.

Even this is not all. The New Testament indicates that he existed before he lived on earth as a historical character. We are thus encouraged to ask not only, 'What was the mode of this earlier existence of his?' (which is part of the question about the person of Christ) but also, 'What is he said to have done in that earlier existence?'. The Bible offers us quite a surprising range of answers to this question.

There are different ways in which this subject could be tackled. The way adopted here is to look first at the evidence of individual biblical authors, or groups of authors. Then, when we have considered what they have to say, we shall see if their accounts are sufficiently in agreement with one another for us to sum up what the Bible as a whole teaches about the various aspects of the work of Jesus.

1

'MY FATHER'S BUSINESS'

The well-known words of the Authorized Version in which Jesus, at the age of twelve, reminded his mother that he must be about his Father's business (Luke 2:49) may not be the best translation. Perhaps what he meant was 'I must be in my Father's house' – 'Where else would you have expected me to be than in my Father's house?'. But even if the words 'I must be about my Father's business' do not convey his meaning on that occasion, they sum up very well his public activity during the last two or three years of his life on earth.

This is repeatedly emphasized in the gospel of John. There Jesus says at an early stage of his ministry, 'My food is to do the will of him who sent me, and to accomplish his work' (John 4:34), while at the end of his ministry he can tell his Father, 'I glorified thee on earth, having accomplished the work which thou gavest me to do' (John 17:4).

'You are my Son'

In some treatments of Christian doctrine the work of Christ does not include an account of his earthly ministry; but there is no good reason for this omission. The earthly ministry was certainly part of the work of Christ, and even if we understand the work of Christ strictly to mean the work of the Messiah, Jesus' earthly ministry was undoubtedly one aspect of his messianic ministry. When Peter, in the house of Cornelius at Caesarea, tells 'how God anointed Jesus of Nazareth with the Holy Spirit and with power' (Acts 10:38), that is as much as to say that God made him Messiah (the anointed one). The anointing in question was his baptism in Jordan by John the Baptist. At his baptism he received a special endowment of the Spirit to equip him for the ministry on which he was about to enter – a ministry which Peter, in the next words he spoke to Cornelius and his friends (Acts 10:38), summed up by describing 'how he went about doing good and healing all that were oppressed by the devil, for God was with him'.

To restrict the work of Christ to his death and its sequel is to make a distinction – between his death and the ministry that preceded it – which the Bible does not make. His death was the crown of his ministry. If his ministry was inaugurated by his baptism in water, it reached its climax in a baptism of another kind, for more than once, looking forward to his death, Jesus spoke of it figuratively as the baptism which he had yet to undergo. His ministry, in word and action alike, proclaimed the kingdom of God, and nowhere was the essence of that kingdom more fully embodied than in him who said to his Father, 'Not my will, but thine, be done' (Luke 22:42), and accepted the cross in that spirit.

From one point of view, Jesus' baptism by John may be regarded as his public dedication to do the will of God. Matthew's account makes this quite explicit. When John showed reluctance to baptize Jesus, saying that it would be more fitting for Jesus to baptize him, Jesus replied in words which are admirably rendered by the New English Bible: 'Let it be so for the present; we do well to conform in this way with all that God requires' (Matthew 3:15). He recognized John's ministry as a work of God and wished to identify himself with it. True, John's baptism was a 'baptism of repentance for the forgiveness of sins' (Mark 1:4) and Jesus had no consciousness of sin. Yet there may be significance in this symbolic association of himself with sinners at the beginning of his ministry, when we consider how, at the end of his ministry, he 'was numbered with the transgressors' and 'bore the sin of many' (in fulfilment of Isaiah 53:12).

If Jesus publicly dedicated himself in this way to do his

Father's will, then we hear the Father's response in the words of the 'voice from heaven' which came to Jesus immediately after his baptism. 'He saw the heavens rent apart', says Mark, using a vivid expression to indicate that now an answer was being given to a prayer uttered by the people hundreds of years before: 'O that thou wouldst rend the heavens and come down!' (Isaiah 64:1). God was now to be actively at work on earth in the ministry of his Son. The heavenly voice which Jesus heard at the same moment said to him, 'You are my Son, my beloved one; with you I am well pleased' (Mark 1:10, 11).

God might well express his pleasure in one who dedicated himself to the doing of his will on earth. But the words in which his pleasure was expressed carried to Jesus a message of their own. 'You are my Son,' in Psalm 2:7 is an oracle addressed by God to his anointed one (his Messiah), the prince of the house of David. 'My beloved one, with whom I am well pleased,' is part of God's introduction in Isaiah 42:1 of one whom he calls 'my servant'. In other words, Jesus knew himself to be hailed by God as the promised Messiah of Israel, but he knew at the same time that his role as the Messiah would have to be fulfilled by the kind of ministry assigned to the Servant in Isaiah 42 and later chapters of the same book – a ministry of obedience in humility and suffering – and not by the way of political power and military conquest which was widely envisaged in messianic expectation.

The descent of the dove

It was while he heard the heavenly voice that Jesus simultaneously received the Spirit – descending on him 'like a dove', as all four gospels say. An endowment of the Spirit was associated in the prophetic writings both with the Messiah and with the Servant of the Lord. Of the coming prince of the house of David it was foretold, 'the Spirit of the LORD shall rest upon him' (Isaiah 11:2); when God introduces his Servant he says, 'Behold my servant ... I have put my Spirit upon him' (Isaiah 42:1). It was fitting then that Jesus, in whom both roles were united, should receive this special endowment with the Spirit of God.

He not only received the Spirit for himself; he received the authority to impart the Spirit to others. Before Jesus' baptism, John had spoken of the coming one for whom he was preparing the way, one stronger than himself for whom he was unworthy to perform the lowliest service. 'I have baptized you with water,' said John to his hearers; 'but he will baptize you with the Holy Spirit' (Mark 1:8). When he spoke these words, John did not know the identity of the coming one; it was the sign from heaven that attended Jesus' baptism that showed him that Jesus was the one who was to fulfil his prophecy.

In the event, Jesus' imparting of the Spirit to others did not take place until he had finished his earthly ministry – until, to use his own language, he had undergone his baptism of death. But when John spelt out what he understood by the baptism with the Spirit which the coming one would administer, he spoke in terms of a ministry of judgement. 'His winnowing fork is in his hand, to clear his threshing floor, and to gather the wheat into his granary, but the chaff he will burn with unquenchable fire.' (Luke 3:17.) There was little enough in Jesus' actual ministry that corresponded to this description – and this was to cause John some perplexity later on.

But we should seriously consider the possibility (and I should put it higher than a mere possibility) that Jesus deliberately absorbed in himself the baptism of judgement which, according to John, was to be administered by the coming one. This would help us to understand why he spoke of his impending suffering and death as a baptism which he had to endure, for in his suffering and death he voluntarily accepted the judgement or retribution which the sins of others had incurred.

Testing in the wilderness

Immediately after he received his messianic commission Jesus' fidelity to it was subjected to its first test. He had been acclaimed by God as his Son. If, then, he was the Son of God, was he to exploit that relationship for his own advantage – by performing a miracle, for example, to relieve his hunger after spending forty days in the wilderness? Was he to force the hand of God – testing him to see if he really meant what he said – by throwing himself down from a height, for example, and expecting God to break his fall by supernatural intervention? Was not this, perhaps, what was meant by the scripture (Psalm 91:11, 12):

> For he will give his angels charge of you
>   to guard you in all your ways;
> on their hands they will bear you up,
>   lest you dash your foot against a stone.

No, it was not; on the contrary, such an action would be an instance of putting God to the test because of refusal to take him at his word, which the Israelites had been condemned for doing in another wilderness centuries before (Deuteronomy 6:16). Jesus had no doubt about the source of these temptations: they came from Satan, that malignant spirit who seduced human beings into disobeying God and then denounced them to God for their disobedience.

Equally, there could be no question of his responding to a further, and specially subtle temptation. 'You are the Son of God,' said the tempter in effect; 'that is, you are the Messiah, the one to whom world dominion has been promised. Think of all the good you can do when world dominion is yours. Even if it involves the use of force, which is foreign to your principles, the end will justify the means. You can put down oppression and injustice wherever it is found; you can establish universal righteousness and peace. But there is only one way to secure world dominion: it is in my gift, and you must pay me homage if you would make it yours.'

Jesus was not the first or the last to have this offer made to him: many had heard it before and many have heard it since, and most of them have fallen for it. What made Jesus turn it down out of hand? He may have recalled that the words 'You are my Son' in Psalm 2 are followed by the promise (verse 8):

Ask of me, and I will make the nations your heritage,
    and the ends of the earth your possession.

If world dominion was to be his, he would receive it from his
Father's hand and from no one else's. In any case, the heavenly
voice had shown him that his messianic destiny was to be
attained by the way of obedient and humble service, and not
by such a way as the tempter was likely to map out for him.
So he dismissed the suggestion with the words of scripture:
'You shall pay homage to the Lord your God, and serve him
alone' (Deuteronomy 6:13).

This particular temptation was to recur more than once in
the course of his ministry, but his prompt repudiation of it on
this first occasion made it easier for him to recognize it and
repel it when it was presented to him later in other forms.

The good news of the kingdom

His wholehearted acceptance of his commission having thus
been tested and proved, Jesus 'returned in the power of the
Spirit into Galilee', as Luke puts it (Luke 4:14), and began to
announce publicly that the appointed time for the approach of
God's kingdom had now come. Generations earlier the prophet
Daniel had told how, after successive pagan empires had run
their course, the God of heaven would set up a kingdom which
would never be superseded but would endure for ever. This
kingdom would be bestowed by him on a human figure – 'one
like a son of man' – in close association with the 'saints of the
Most High' (Daniel 7:13, 18). When Jesus spoke of 'the Son
of Man', he meant that 'one like a son of man' whom Daniel
had seen in his vision; and as for the 'saints of the Most High',
he made their identity plain when he said to his disciples, 'Fear
not, little flock, for it is your Father's good pleasure to give
you the kingdom' (Luke 12:32).

But one who proclaims a kingdom in terms like these must
be expected to do something about setting it up. Teaching
and action were combined in Jesus' ministry, and the teaching

and the action together showed what the nature of this new kingdom was.

There were many voices in Israel at that time proclaiming the coming kingdom in terms of militant nationalism. Judas the Galilean, who had led a rising against the Roman administration of Judaea when Jesus was a boy, had come to grief, but his soul went marching on. His followers still maintained that it was wrong for the Jewish people to pay taxes to the Roman emperor, and asserted that, if only they would rise with a will against the Romans, God would help their enterprise and enable them to drive the hated imperialists out.

The way of Jesus was quite different. It was not the self-assertive who would inherit the kingdom, he said, but the humble, the meek, the merciful, the pure in heart and the peacemakers. Sorrow and suffering might be their lot at present, but they would receive a great reward. Meanwhile, the right policy was not forceful resistance but submission – turning the other cheek and going the second mile.

When was a kingdom ever established by such means as these? And when did a subject nation ever gain its freedom from oppressors by meek submission? Jesus was turning the accepted principles of political action upside down; strictly speaking, he was being much more revolutionary than the militant nationalists. They tried to overthrow their oppressors by using their oppressors' weapons and methods – and they failed. Jesus followed in practice the way he recommended in preaching – and he won. His disciples followed the same way throughout two and a half centuries of persecution – and they also won. (Then, having won, they began to forget the lesson they had learned – but that is another story.)

A question and its answer

John the Baptist was not a militant nationalist. But even he found something strange in the reports that came to him about what Jesus was saying and doing. He could not go and hear for himself, for he was in prison. He had been arrested and

locked up by one of the Herods, the ruler of Galilee and some
territory east of the Jordan, for denouncing Herod's second
marriage as disobedience to the law of God (since his second
wife's former husband, his own half-brother, was still alive).
But John's disciples were able to come and visit him in prison,
and he sent two of them to Jesus with the question: 'Are you
really the coming one, or must we look for someone else?'
(Luke 7:19.) John had foretold a ministry of judgement for the
coming one, and by all accounts this was not the kind of
ministry that Jesus was engaged in. John had proclaimed Jesus
as the coming one: had he been mistaken? And perhaps another
question rose in John's mind: 'If he is really the coming one,
why does he not do something for me in my imprisonment?'

So John's disciples came to Jesus with their master's question.
Jesus might have said to them, 'Yes; go back and tell John that
I am certainly the coming one.' But that would scarcely have
satisfied John, who might have said to himself, 'Ah, but perhaps
he himself is mistaken!' Jesus gave John's messengers a better
answer than that. 'You stay here and watch,' he said to them.

They stayed and watched. And as they did so, says Luke,
Jesus 'cured many of diseases and plagues and evil spirits, and
on many that were blind he bestowed sight' (Luke 7:21). Then
he said to them (verse 22),

> Go and tell John what you have seen and heard: the blind receive
> their sight, the lame walk, lepers are cleansed, and the deaf hear,
> the dead are raised up, the poor have good news preached to them.

And, he added (verse 23), tell him this from me: 'Blessed is
the man who doesn't think that I have let him down.'

When the two disciples went back to John, he would have
got the message all right. Sight for the blind, hearing for the
deaf, strength for the cripple – these were the very things that
the prophets had said would mark the new age when it came,
and these were the very things that Jesus was doing! John could
have called to mind a prophecy like that in Isaiah 35:5–6:

> Then the eyes of the blind shall be opened,
>   and the ears of the deaf unstopped;

then shall the lame man leap like a hart,
and the tongue of the dumb sing for joy,

and he would have recognized that this was exactly what was happening now.

And as for the bringing of good news to the poor, there was another passage in the same book (Isaiah 61:1–2), which Jesus on another occasion applied to himself:

The Spirit of the Lord God is upon me,
because the Lord has anointed me
to bring good news to the poor [*or* afflicted];
he has sent me to bind up the broken-hearted,
to proclaim liberty to the captives,
and release to those who are fettered;
to proclaim the acceptable year of the Lord.

The prophet goes on immediately to add, 'and the day of vengeance of our God'; but when Jesus read this passage one sabbath day early on in his ministry in the synagogue of Nazareth, he stopped short at 'the acceptable year of the LORD'. If he had gone on to read 'and the day of vengeance of our God', he could not have begun his following address by saying, as he did, 'Today this scripture has been fulfilled in your hearing' (Luke 4:21). For he had come as the messenger, and indeed the embodiment of God's favour, not of his vengeance. John the Baptist might have wished to hear from his messengers at least something about 'the day of vengeance of our God', but he heard enough to assure him that Jesus was indeed the coming one. He had not been mistaken; Jesus had not let him down.

Works of mercy and power

The works of mercy and power which marked Jesus' ministry – his miracles, as they are commonly called – were not simply wonders performed in order to impress his hearers with his authority. They gave evidence of his authority, of course, but so did his words. Whereas the prophets in earlier days said 'Thus says the Lord' and the scribes of his own day quoted revered teachers of a past generation, here was one who was content to say, '*I* say to you,' sometimes solemnly emphasizing these words by prefacing 'Amen' – meaning 'in truth' or, as the older English versions rendered it, 'verily'. His words and his deeds were all of a piece. A poet does not write poetry to prove that he is a poet; he writes it because he is a poet. So Jesus performed his mighty works not to prove that he was the Son of God but because he was the Son of God. They were, as someone has put it, not the seals on the document guaranteeing its genuineness; they were part of the text itself. That is to say, they were as much part of the message of the kingdom of God as the teaching was. If the teaching was largely given in spoken parables, the mighty works were acted parables, setting forth the same lessons.

There was a rival kingdom to the kingdom of God, and that was the kingdom of darkness and sin, whose agents were spiritual forces. The announcement of the imminence of God's kingdom caused consternation among those forces, which had formerly dominated the minds of many men and women and now saw their domination threatened. This led to a redoubling of their activity in human life, which explains why so many of Jesus' acts of healing took the form of expelling demons from those whom they controlled. Many of the conditions which the gospels describe in these terms would be described otherwise by psychiatrists and other medical specialists today, but the fact that they are now referred to by a different vocabulary does not diminish their reality. If we refer to them in the vocabulary which the gospels use we shall see more clearly their relevance to Jesus' message of the kingdom. Any form of disease or premature death in God's world was an affront to his love, but this form of illness was the greatest affront of all, because it was evidence of the determination of the powers of evil not to yield to the new kingdom without a struggle.

Jesus summed up the situation by means of a short parable: 'When a strong man, fully armed, guards his own palace, his goods are in peace; but when one stronger than himself attacks him and overcomes him, he takes away his armour in which he trusted, and divides his goods as plunder' (Luke 11:21–22). The 'strong man' was the chief ruler of the kingdom of evil, whom the Jews in their language called Beelzebul (meaning something like 'lord of the palace'). His palace had formerly been secure, but now the stronger power of the kingdom of God in the person of Jesus was breaking into his palace, binding him, seizing his property and, best of all, releasing his captives. This was a sure sign that the kingdom of God was at work. 'If it is by the Spirit of God that I cast out demons,' said Jesus, 'then the kingdom of God has come upon you.' (Matthew 12:28.)

Some of the leaders in Israel were unwilling to acknowledge the divine authority by which Jesus acted, and put his mighty works down to the power of Beelzebul operating through him. This was a manifest absurdity, as it was the power of Beelzebul that was being broken by Jesus' works. But if men who ought to have known better closed their eyes to the light and refused to admit the evidence of the Spirit of God at work among them, then there was no hope for them. (This is what is meant by the unpardonable sin, which has caused much unnecessary anxiety to some people of tender conscience.)

Some of Jesus' mighty works took the form of control over other aspects of nature than human life and health. When he quieted the storm on the lake of Galilee his disciples were filled with awe, and said, 'Who then is this, that even wind and sea obey him?' (Mark 4:41). The story is told in such a way as to suggest that he commanded the power which God had displayed in his works of creation and in delivering his people from Egypt. When the Creator caused the dry land to emerge from the water, he curbed the unruly sea and said, 'Thus far shall you come, and no farther, and here shall your proud waves be stayed' (Job 38:11). When he caused the water of the Red Sea (or rather 'the sea of reeds') to recede so as to let the Israelites escape from Egypt, he exerted the same power. Now Jesus exerts it too and lets it be seen that the creative and delivering power of God is at his disposal. Not only so, but

Jesus' power to control the outward raging of natural forces was matched immediately afterwards by his power to control the inward raging of human passion in his healing of the Gadarene demoniac (Mark 5:1–20).

The feeding of the multitude in the wilderness (Mark 6:30–44) again showed that the power of God, who had fed his people in another wilderness during their pilgrimage from Egypt to the promised land, was at work in Jesus. The gospel of John makes it plain that Jesus' feeding of the five thousand with loaves and fishes, like God's feeding of the Israelites with manna in Moses' day, was an object-lesson pointing (in John Masefield's words) to

> the holy bread
> By which the soul of man is fed,
> The holy bread, the food unpriced,
> Thine everlasting mercy, Christ!

The lesson taught by the miraculous feeding is summed up thus by Jesus: 'I am the bread of life; he who comes to me shall not hunger, and he who believes in me shall never thirst.' (John 6:35.)

'You are the Messiah'

Jesus' feeding of the multitude was the occasion for the renewal of one of his earlier temptations – the temptation to fulfil his messianic mission by another course than that which was the Father's will for him. The five thousand men who had been fed were a potential army looking for a captain – that is probably what Jesus meant when he described them as 'sheep without a shepherd' (Mark 6:34). Now, they thought, they had found the captain for whom they were looking; they tried to take Jesus by force and make him their king, to lead them against the Roman oppressors and their creatures, the Herods (John 6:15). The situation was a delicate one: Jesus could not trust his own closest disciples, who were in danger of being infected by the crowd's militant enthusiasm, and he had to compel them to embark in their boat and cross to the other side of the lake of Galilee, while he stayed behind and persuaded the crowd to disperse.

They did disperse, but many of them felt disillusioned. Here was a potential leader with obvious power at his disposal: if only he would consent to use that power in the national interest, nothing could stand in his way. But when he refused to seize such a golden opportunity, many had no further use for him. This crisis marked the end of his popularity in Galilee.

Taking his disciples away from Galilee, out of reach of the nationalist influences to which they were so ready to respond, he taught them more of the true nature of his messianic mission, in which they had their part to play. At last he tested their understanding of his teaching, and asked them who they thought he really was. When Peter, acting as spokesman for his companions, said, 'You are the Messiah,' this was a significant confession. If Jesus was the Messiah, it meant that a radical change had come about in their previous ideas of the sort of person the Messiah was and the kind of things he would do. For Jesus did not correspond to popular ideas about the Messiah, and showed no sign of undertaking the kind of programme which many hoped the Messiah would accomplish.

Peter's confession thus gave evidence of a shift – or at least the beginnings of a shift – in the picture of the Messiah held by him and the other disciples. But he and they had a long way to go yet, and this became clear almost immediately.

It was now that Jesus began to talk to them plainly about what lay in store for him: not worldly triumph and coronation, but repudiation, suffering and death: 'the Son of Man must suffer many things, and be rejected' (Mark 8:31). If they thought they were following him to national liberation and the eager acclaim of a grateful people, let them think again. To follow him meant taking up the cross – and 'taking up the cross' was no empty figure of speech in first-century Palestine.

Whatever new conception of messianic destiny they had begun to associate with their Master, it was nothing like this. The first time he spoke to them in these terms Peter, who had

just confessed him to be the Messiah, took him by the arm
and said earnestly, 'God bless you, Master! This is never going
to happen to you!' Jesus replied to this well-meant expostulation
with what must have been surprising severity: 'Get behind me,
Satan! These are men's thoughts, not God's.' (Mark 8:33.)

What did he mean? He certainly did not identify Peter with
the personal devil. No, but he recognized in Peter's well-
intentioned remonstrance the same old temptation as he had
encountered and resisted in the wilderness – the temptation
to achieve his messianic destiny by another way than the
Servant's way of rejection and suffering. He repelled it now
with the same words as he had used to repel it then. Nothing
must turn him aside from completing 'his Father's business'.

From this point on, the way of Jesus' ministry becomes more
and more clearly the way of the cross.

2

THE WAY OF THE CROSS

At quite an early stage in his ministry Jesus began to find himself at odds with the religious and political authorities.

Conflict with the religious authorities

Conflict with the religious authorities arose first of all from his insistence on healing people on the sabbath day, even during synagogue services. The law of the sabbath was laid down in the fourth of the ten commandments. The fourth commandment directed the Israelites not to do any work on the sabbath day. At one time everyone had a fairly clear idea of what was meant by 'work' in this sense, but with changes in conditions of life it became necessary to define 'work' more precisely. In some Jewish teaching there were set forth thirty-nine forms of activity which were to be regarded as 'work' forbidden on the sabbath day. For example, reaping grain and grinding it were two of these activities. When fault was found with Jesus' disciples for plucking ears of grain as they walked through the fields on the sabbath and rubbing them between their hands to extract the kernel, it was because plucking was reckoned to be a form of reaping, and rubbing a form of grinding.

As for healing people on the sabbath, the exponents of the law were not unreasonable. If it was a matter of life or death, if delay would be dangerous, then by all means, they agreed, the saving of life should take precedence over the sabbath law. But if sick or disabled persons could easily wait until sunset, when the new day officially started, then let them wait.

But Jesus said, 'Why should they wait?' A law of God could best be obeyed by the fulfilment of the purpose for which it was given. Now the sabbath was given for the rest and relief of human beings, and anything which promoted that end was a proper thing to do on the sabbath. By curing people he gave them rest and relief from disease and pain, and the sabbath was the most fitting day for such activity.

This reasoning was persuasive and attractive, but many of the religious leaders found it subversive. Jesus, in their eyes, had no authority to act or teach as he did; he was under-mining established authority and was a dangerous influence.

In Galilee and Jerusalem alike it was this attitude of his towards the sabbath that first involved him in conflict. John tells in his gospel how Jesus, during a visit to Jerusalem, cured a cripple on the sabbath day at the Pool of Bethesda. When he was challenged for his alleged breach of the law of God, he gave an astounding reply: 'My Father is working still, and I am working.' (John 5:17.)

This reply might well have reminded his hearers of a subject which lent itself to grave debate. Did God himself desist from all work on the sabbath day, as his people were commanded to do? True, when creation's work was finished, the scriptural narrative told how 'he rested on the seventh day from all his work which he had done' (Genesis 2:2). But it was plain that, when he rested from his creative work, he did not rest from his work of providence, from maintaining the creation in being, either then or on any subsequent sabbath day. If he did, then inevitably the universe would dissolve into nothingness, and would have to be created all over again at the beginning of each new week. So, it was generally agreed, God kept on working all the time, sabbath day or no sabbath day.

What made Jesus' reply so astounding, however, was that he claimed this example of God as a precedent for himself to follow. Not only so, but he spoke of God as 'my Father' in a way which suggested that he stood in a special relation to God. What the Son sees the Father doing, it is his right and indeed his duty to do. If the Son sees the Father working on the sabbath, it is for him to work on the sabbath too. But this, his hearers decided, was intolerable; he was in effect putting himself on a level with God. This was as near to blasphemy as made no difference, and blasphemy was a capital offence in Jewish law. His bold claim was not forgotten; it was brought up against him on each subsequent occasion when he visited Jerusalem for one or another of the great festivals, and on his last visit it figured in his trial and condemnation.

Conflict with Herod Antipas

It was not only with the religious authorities that Jesus came into conflict. In Galilee, where he proclaimed the new kingdom and performed so many of his mighty works, the ruler there became more and more suspicious of him and his companions. This was Herod Antipas, who had imprisoned John the Baptist and later ordered his execution. Now it seemed to Herod that in Jesus he was faced with another John the Baptist, and that he might have to take the same drastic measures against him. Apart from anything else, Herod was held responsible by the Roman emperor for maintaining peace in his principality, and he could not afford to risk any movement which might develop into a popular rising. He had his informants everywhere, and would know all about those who envisaged Jesus as the military leader for whom so many were waiting. When Jesus sent his disciples out two by two to announce the good news of the coming kingdom in the towns and villages of Galilee, Herod would hear of the excitement which their mission caused. The feeding of the multitude, after which an attempt was made to compel Jesus to assume the kingship, took place on the east side of the lake of Galilee, outside Herod's territory, but the men who made the attempt were Herod's subjects. No wonder that some well-disposed Pharisees warned Jesus to get out of Galilee, for, they said, 'Herod wants to kill you' (Luke 13:31). This was the occasion which called forth Jesus' description of Herod as 'that fox'. He was not greatly alarmed by the warning. Herod could not touch him before his work was done, and even then it was not in Herod's territory that he would face the final crisis: 'it would never do for a prophet to perish away from Jerusalem'.

Nevertheless he did leave Galilee at that time and took his disciples out of Herod's reach to give them the instruction that was necessary to prepare them for what lay ahead of them on their next visit to Jerusalem. The territory through which they passed at this time mostly belonged to Herod's brother Philip ('Philip the tetrarch'), but the majority of Philip's subjects were Gentiles, and there was not the same danger of Jewish national enthusiasm boiling over there as there was in Galilee. Philip's capital was at Caesarea Philippi, near one of the sources of the Jordan, and it was in that neighbourhood that Peter made his historic confession of Jesus as the Messiah.

Conflict in Jerusalem

As we have seen, Peter's confession gave Jesus the cue to tell his disciples about his impending rejection and death, and not long afterwards he and his disciples set out on the road to Jerusalem, the most appropriate place in the world (as he said) for a prophet to meet his fate. Jerusalem must hear the good news of the kingdom of God as Galilee had heard it, but Jesus had no illusions about the reception which Jerusalem was likely to give to him and his message. If his message were accepted, it would prove to be the way of peace, but there were forces at work in Jerusalem which would lead to the rejection of the way of peace and thus ensure the ruin of the city and its inhabitants.

The Jewish authorities themselves were well aware of those forces, which were set on a collision course with the Roman military occupation. Those Jewish authorities, at whose head stood the chief priests, were desperately anxious to hold the rebellious forces at bay. Their own position, they knew, depended on the maintenance of peaceful relations with the Roman administration, and if those peaceful relations were disrupted, they themselves would be swept away in the ensuing catastrophe.

But they were far from recognizing an ally in Jesus with his message of peace. There was, indeed, nothing in common between Jesus' policy of repaying evil with good and the conviction held by the militant patriots that the only good Roman was a dead one. But Jesus was the sort of leader who attracted a following of the common people, and however innocent his own motives might be, such a following as he attracted was likely to arouse the suspicion of the Romans. Public safety might therefore require that Jesus should be put out of harm's way.

Jesus spent some time teaching in the temple precincts during the week of the Feast of Tabernacles in the autumn of A.D. 29, and again during the Feast of Dedication at mid-winter, but the crowds that thronged him during those festivals provided a kind of bodyguard which made it inexpedient to take any action against him. For the next three months Jesus withdrew with his disciples to a quiet spot in the wilderness of Judaea. From there he emerged briefly to provide urgently needed help to a family at Bethany, near Jerusalem, with whom he had enjoyed hospitality on his visits to the capital. Lazarus, a member of the family, had died, and Jesus' action in calling him out of the rock-tomb in which he had been interred, and restoring him alive to his two sisters, inevitably made a tremendous impression in the whole area.

When, therefore, the Feast of Passover approached a few weeks later and Jesus went to Jerusalem for the last time, he was escorted by a cheering band of pilgrims who clearly thought that the kingdom of God was on the point of being established. Indeed it was, but in quite a different sense from anything that they envisaged. The chief priests' apprehensions seemed to them to be only too well founded. Jesus himself was mounted on a donkey, not a war-horse; he came in peace and not with armed force. But it was all too easy for such a crowd to get out of hand.

Evidently, however, there was nothing about his entry into Jerusalem which moved the Romans to intervene. A crowd of unarmed countryfolk escorting a man riding on a donkey, waving branches and clothes about and yelling their heads off, did not seem to present any military threat. Even when Jesus went into the outer court of the temple the following day and drove out the cattle-dealers and money-changers who had recently – and perhaps only temporarily – installed themselves there, the Romans took no action. They would certainly have done so if this had been a demonstration of mob-violence. There was a strong Roman garrison in the Antonia fortress, adjoining the temple on the north-west and communicating with the outer court by two flights of steps. If any riotous behaviour broke out in the temple precincts, a detachment of troops would be down at the double and a few sword-thrusts to right and left would quickly have dispersed the rioters. Indeed, something of the sort took place a few months earlier, to judge by the reference in Luke 13:1 to certain Galileans 'whose blood Pilate [the Roman governor of Judaea] had mingled with their sacrifices'. That incident must have taken place in the Jerusalem temple, for that was the only place where sacrifices could be offered. But on this occasion there was no Roman intervention – plainly because the situation did not seem to call for it.

Jesus' cleansing of the temple was not intended to be an act of violence, whether against the temple itself, the Jewish establishment, or the Roman occupation. It was the kind of 'prophetic action' which prophets in earlier days had sometimes performed to drive home more forcibly their spoken messages. 'Is it not written,' Jesus protested (quoting Isaiah 56:7), '"My house shall be called a house of prayer for all the nations"? But,' he added (quoting from another prophet, see page 33), 'you have made it a den of robbers.' The outer court of the temple was sometimes called the court of the Gentiles. Gentiles were strictly debarred from entering the inner courts, which were accessible to Jews only; but they might come into the outer court and worship the true God there. If, however, the place where they might do so was taken up by traders and money-changers, then they were being robbed of their opportunity of approaching God and God was being robbed of their worship.

When Jesus said that the house of God had been turned into a den of robbers, he echoed language used by the prophet

Jeremiah in the name of God over 600 years before, with regard
to Solomon's temple: 'Has this house, which is called by my
name, become a den of robbers in your eyes?' (Jeremiah 7:11).
Jeremiah had warned his hearers that the temple which they
were desecrating would be destroyed – as indeed it was, by the
Babylonians a few years later. In Jesus' protest there was at
least the implication that a similar fate lay in store for that even
more glorious temple in which he then stood. Jeremiah's words
nearly cost him his life, and Jesus might be incurring a similar
risk. A day or two later he sat with some of his disciples on
the slope of Mount Olivet, looking across to the temple area
with its magnificent buildings, and told them that the time was
approaching when not one stone would be left standing on
another; all would be demolished. His disciples would not be
the only people to hear what he said. When Judaea became
a Roman province in A.D. 6, the Romans deprived the Jewish
authorities of the right to inflict capital punishment – except
with regard to offences against the sanctity of the temple,
whether by deed or by word.

The question of taxation

Another change that came about when Judaea was reorganized
as a Roman province in A.D. 6 was that its inhabitants had to
pay their taxes direct to the imperial exchequer in Rome. Taxes
were burdensome no matter to whom they were paid, and the
public tax-collectors were often quite unscrupulous in extorting
more than they should from the taxpayers. We need not suppose
that Galileans paid less tax to Herod Antipas than Judaeans
paid to the emperor, but at least Herod Antipas was a Jew,
while the emperor was a pagan. When the new order imposed
in A.D. 6 required the Judaeans to pay taxes to the emperor,
Judas the Galilean proclaimed a doctrine that had not been
heard in Jewish circles before – that for them, the chosen people
of God, to pay taxes to a pagan ruler was sacrilege. Judas led
a rising which was quickly put down by Roman soldiers, but
his doctrine lived on. It was a congenial doctrine. No one liked

having to pay taxes to Rome, and it was good to think that this dislike had a sound religious basis. Of course they had to continue paying taxes to Rome whether they liked it or not, whether it was pleasing to heaven or not; if any reluctance was shown, the Romans had ruthless methods of compulsion. But the question was always sure to arouse animated discussion, and the patriotism and (from some points of view) the orthodoxy of a visiting teacher could be tested by his attitude on this point.

Naturally, then, while Jesus was teaching in the temple precincts two or three days after his arrival in Jerusalem, a deputation waited on him to put this question to him. 'Is it lawful to pay taxes to Caesar, or not? Should we pay them, or should we not?' When they said 'Is is lawful?' they were referring not (of course) to Roman law, which demanded payment, but to the law of God.

Was Jesus to answer yes or no? If he said yes, he would lose much of his current popularity. If he said no, he could be denounced to Pilate, the Roman governor, for fomenting sedition; and there could be only one outcome to such a denunciation. 'Let me see a coin,' he said, meaning the silver Roman coin, about the size of a shilling (5p) or a quarter, and called a *denarius*. (It was in Roman coinage that the imperial taxes were paid.) 'Now,' he said, when one was produced, 'whose face is this? Whose name is this?' Just as British coins bear the face and name of the monarch, so a Roman *denarius* bore the face and name of Caesar (as every Roman emperor was called). To his question there could be only one answer: the coin bore Caesar's face and name. 'Well,' said he, 'give Caesar back what belongs to him; but see to it that you give God what is due to *him*.' (Mark 12:13–17.)

Perhaps his answer implied that a truly pious Jew should not have such a coin on his person: because it bore Caesar's image it infringed the second commandment, which forbade 'any likeness of anything that is in heaven above, or that is in the earth beneath' (Exodus 20:4). There were some scrupulously religious Jews who would not even look at such a coin, let alone possess one. We cannot be sure if Jesus had this in mind. He

did mean that the claims of God upon his people would not
be diminished if Caesar were to be given money which so
obviously belonged to him. Caesar's money was properly used
in paying Caesar's taxes but, as Jesus had said during his
Galilean ministry, God's kingdom and righteousness should be
sought first, and then everything else would fall into its proper
place.

Certainly Jesus said nothing on this delicate subject which
could form the basis of a charge against him before the Roman
governor. But he may well have lost the good will of many of
the bystanders, whether they were residents in Jerusalem or
pilgrims up from Galilee. The hopes of a coup which some
of them had cherished when they shouted 'Hosanna' at his entry
into the city had now evaporated. They may have expected
him then to lead them into the temple precincts, and institute
the new kingdom by taking over the holy area in the name of
God. He had done no such thing. His 'cleansing' of the temple
was probably popular enough, but it was not directed against
the Romans. And now, by refusing to denounce the payment
of taxes to Caesar, he had shown clearly that he was not the
leader they wanted. They were completely disillusioned in him,
as the militant Galileans had been when he refused to be their
king after the feeding of the multitude.

The last supper

Even if popular support for him was waning, the chief priests
did not think it wise to take any action against him during the
festival season. If a riot were inadvertently sparked off, they
would be bringing about the very crisis they were so anxious
to avoid. But, for some inexplicable reason, one of Jesus'
disciples, Judas Iscariot, secured an audience with them a couple
of days before the passover, and undertook to enable them to
arrest Jesus quietly, in circumstances where there would be no
risk of a riot.

Jesus knew very well that there was a traitor in the camp,
and planned his movements for the next twenty-four hours with

special care. He could see the danger which was closing in on him, but he had resolved to keep the passover with his disciples for one last time before he was arrested. There were some variations in calculating the calendar at that time, and there are grounds for thinking that he kept the passover with his disciples twenty-four hours before the official date. However that may be, he had made the necessary arrangements to keep it in the upper room of a trusted friend in Jerusalem, and on the appointed evening he met his twelve chief disciples there.

The passover commemorated a great deliverance which the God of Israel had accomplished for his people more than a thousand years before. The celebrants did their best to imagine themselves in the place of their ancestors observing the first passover on the eve of their escape from Egypt. Thus, when they were about to eat the unleavened bread which formed an essential part of the meal, the head of the family or leader of the company said: 'This is the bread of affliction which our fathers ate when they came out of Egypt.' On this occasion, however, Jesus gave a new significance to the bread when he took it from the table, gave thanks to God for it, broke it and gave it to his disciples with the words: 'Take it; this is my body.'

When a blessing was said at the end of the meal, it was customary to share a cup of wine which was called 'the cup of blessing'. When they were about to do so on this occasion, Jesus took the cup and, after saying the blessing over it, gave it to his disciples. 'This is my covenant blood,' he told them, 'which is poured out for many. In truth I tell you, I shall not drink the fruit of the vine again until I drink it new in the kingdom of God.' (Mark 14:22–25.)

What the disciples could have understood by those words at the time is difficult to decide. In the light of the events which were to follow immediately afterwards, the words and the accompanying actions acquired a much fuller significance for them than they could have had at that supper-table. But if we can discover what Jesus meant by them, we may understand in some measure how he viewed his impending death.

If the passover commemorated a great deliverance in the past,

Jesus' words and actions on this occasion were designed to give the supper a new meaning, associated with a new deliverance. The earlier deliverance had been followed by the institution of a solemn covenant between the people of Israel and the God of their fathers, by which he undertook to be their God and they undertook to be his people. Part of that covenant ceremony involved the sacrifice of animals and the shedding of their blood, while Moses said: 'Behold the blood of the covenant which the LORD has made with you in accordance with all these words.' (Exodus 24:8.) 'All these words' were the words of the law which Moses had read to them and which they promised to obey.

Equally, the new deliverance was to be associated with a new covenant, ratified not by the blood of sacrificed animals but by the blood of Jesus – that is, the voluntary surrender of his life on his people's behalf. That is the meaning of his words, 'This is my covenant blood, which is poured out for many,' and similarly he pointed to the deliverance which his death would accomplish for them when he spoke of the bread as his body, given for them.

Jesus clearly foresaw his death at the hands of his enemies. From one point of view it might appear that they had the initiative and that he was their helpless victim. But he was resolved to wrest the initiative from them and make his death a means for the deliverance of many, offering himself up to God for their sake. Thus he, not his enemies, would have the last word. And there in the upper room, while he kept the passover with his disciples, he consecrated himself to God for this purpose.

Arrest, trial and crucifixion

From the upper room Jesus took his disciples across the Kidron valley, east of the city, to a spot on the slope of Olivet where they had been accustomed to foregather on their visits to Jerusalem – a spot well-known to Judas. The final crisis was fast approaching. Jesus would have liked his disciples to be inwardly prepared to meet it, but he knew how unprepared they were. He had told them about it repeatedly in recent weeks and months, but they could not believe that he really meant what he said. Now he urged them to stay awake, and to pray that they might not fail in the test – the crucial test of faith and loyalty to which they would be exposed any minute now. How wonderful it would be if they stood the test and stayed by his side, ready to drink his cup and share his baptism! But when the test came, they deserted him and took to their heels. The spirit, as he told them, was willing, but the flesh was weak. The future of his cause was precarious indeed, if it was to be entrusted to followers like these!

He himself had his final test to face. He had been tested before, and emerged from each test more firmly resolved to do his Father's will and achieve his messianic destiny by the way of the Servant. But now the price of this resolve had to be paid in humiliation and death: was he still prepared to go through with it? Even at this late hour, escape was not impossible, but escape would mean disobedience to the heavenly voice. This was the burden of his agonizing prayer: 'Abba, Father, all things are possible to thee; remove this cup from me; yet not what I will, but what thou wilt.' (Mark 14:36.) As many of his servants have proved since then, such a prayer may be answered not by the removal of the 'cup' with its bitter contents, but by the giving of added grace and power to accept it. This is how it was with Jesus; he rose from his agony strengthened, not weakened. When, almost immediately afterwards, the detachment of temple police, guided by Judas, came to the spot, he submitted to arrest with the words: 'Let the scriptures be fulfilled.' (Mark 14:49.)

John's narrative suggests that Roman auxiliary troops were there as well as the temple police. This reminds us of the animatedly debated question as to who was responsible for Jesus' arrest, trial, condemnation and execution. One thing is certain: crucifixion was a Roman, not a Jewish penalty. Moreover, the charge on which he was sentenced to death, written in three languages on a placard fixed above his head on the cross, was an offence in Roman law, not in Jewish law. The inscription

'The king of the Jews' implied that he laid claim to a sovereignty which was exercised at that time by the Roman emperor – that he was guilty of sedition.

But the chief priests of Jerusalem cannot be exonerated from a share in the responsibility for his death. It appears, indeed, that they acted as his prosecutors before the Roman governor. This, however, does not involve the Jewish people in the same responsibility, as many Christians have foolishly, and tragically, imagined. The chief priests had no option but to be collaborators with the occupying power. We might take as a parallel the plight of Norway under Nazi occupation during the Second World War. There were some Norwegians who collaborated with the occupying forces and were prepared to do some of their dirty work for them: they were headed by one Major Quisling, who has given his name to a particular brand of traitor. He and his associates probably believed, however wrongly, that they were acting in their country's best interests. But no one would dream of holding the Norwegian people as a whole responsible in the slightest degree for the misdeeds of Quisling and his fellow collaborators. It would be equally misguided to hold the Jewish people as a whole responsible in the slightest degree for the action of the high priest Caiaphas and his colleagues in Jerusalem on the first Good Friday.

Jesus was taken before a court of enquiry over which the high priest presided. An attempt was apparently made to convict him of language which amounted to an attack on the sanctity of the temple. He was charged with saying, 'I will destroy this temple that is made with hands, and in three days I will build another, not made with hands' (Mark 14:58). He certainly had said something like this, predicting the replacement of the temple and all that it stood for by the new order which he was to inaugurate. But the rules of evidence in a Jewish court were strict, and the witnesses who reported Jesus' words did not agree, so their testimony collapsed. If it had been admitted and Jesus had been convicted on this charge, then the Jewish authorities would presumably have been able to deal with him according to their own law since, as we have seen, sacrilege against the temple

was an offence for which they were permitted by the Romans
to inflict the death penalty themselves. The death penalty in
that case would no doubt have been stoning, as it actually was
a few years later when Stephen, the first Christian martyr, was
charged with (among other things) continually 'speaking words
against this holy place' (the temple), saying 'that this Jesus
of Nazareth will destroy this place' (Acts 6:13–14).

The court of enquiry had been hastily convened, and no other
witnesses were available. The high priest then directed Jesus
to say whether or not he was the Messiah, the Son of the
Blessed One (God). People had not forgotten his claim, made
on an earlier visit to Jerusalem, to be the Son of God. Jesus
replied to the high priest's question in words which appear to
have meant: 'If "Messiah" is the term you insist on using, then
I can only say that I am; but if I were to choose my own form
of words, this is what I should say: "You shall see the Son
of Man seated at the right hand of the Almighty, and coming
with the clouds of Heaven."' (See Mark 14:62.) That is to say,
the Son of Man, discredited and humiliated as he was then,
would be publicly vindicated by God and would visit mankind
in mercy and judgement. It was as though he appealed from
the judgement of the earthly court to the superior judgement
of the heavenly court.

If on an earlier occasion his claim to be the Son of God had
incurred a charge of blasphemy, the language in which he now
amplified the claim seemed to compound the offence. To speak
of sitting at the right hand of the Almighty was in fact a claim
to be his equal. Conviction for blasphemy was a foregone
conclusion.

While blasphemy was a capital offence by Jewish law, it did
not belong to that restricted area in which the Jewish authorities
retained capital jurisdiction under the Roman administration.
If the death sentence was to be carried out, permission would
have to be secured from the Roman governor who, as it
happened, was at that time resident in Jerusalem. And the
Roman governor was not likely to take seriously a charge of
blasphemy against the God of Israel. However, the claim to

be Messiah had political as well as religious implications. Pilate might not be impressed by a claim to be the Son of God, but a claim to be Israel's Messiah, the king of the Jews, was a different matter.

Instead of rubber-stamping the Jewish court's verdict, Pilate reopened the case as though it were a completely new one. He was satisfied quite soon that the kingship which Jesus claimed posed no threat to Caesar's sovereignty; but Caesar was a suspicious character, and would not look kindly on a governor who showed leniency to one who claimed to be a king in any sense of the word. Sooner than incur the ill will of Caesar, then, Pilate sentenced Jesus to death.

The death-sentence for sedition, in the case of one who was not a Roman citizen, was regularly carried out by crucifixion. But Jesus accepted even this as God's will for him, and the spirit in which he accepted it meant that, instead of bringing his ministry to an abrupt end, it crowned his ministry. The Son of Man who, as he told his disciples, came not to receive service but to give it, consummated his career of service by giving his life as 'a ransom for many' (Mark 10:45).

But no one could have appreciated this at the moment when Jesus breathed his last. By all ordinary calculations of success, Jesus' ministry had ended in a double failure – first a failure in Galilee, when so many of his followers turned away from him, and then a more tragic failure in Jerusalem where, deserted by his disciples and (as it seemed) God-forsaken, he died on the cross. What could be said now about 'the work of Christ'?

3

THE WORK GOES ON

Christ risen and active

What could be said now about 'the work of Christ'? His enemies, who reckoned Jesus to be a false Christ, were glad to think that nothing more would be heard of him or his work. As for his friends, we know what they said: 'we had hoped that he was the one to redeem Israel' (Luke 24:21). That was what two of his disciples said on the road to Emmaus on the third day after his death, as they poured out the story of their grief and disillusionment into the ears of an unrecognized but sympathetic fellow traveller; and they spoke for their fellow disciples too. The bottom had fallen out of their world, one and all.

Then, suddenly, all was well. Jesus, crucified, dead and buried, had risen from the tomb. In the language of the Authorized Version, 'he showed himself alive after his passion' to his disciples 'by many infallible proofs' (Acts 1:3). Their doubts and fears were gone: Jesus was not only alive but powerfully present.

Could the resurrection of Christ be reckoned as an aspect of his work? In some degree it could: he is described as the conqueror or the destroyer of death. The old miracle plays on 'the harrowing of hell' present this achievement of his in dramatic form. Hymn-writers tell the same story in poetic form:

> He hell in hell laid low;
> Made sin, he sin o'erthrew:
> Bowed to the grave, destroyed it so,
> And death, by dying, slew.

When the New Testament writers speak of his resurrection in less pictorial terms, however, they usually refer to it as the work of God. 'God raised him up,' said Peter on the day of Pentecost, 'having loosed the pangs of death, because it was not possible for death to hold him fast' (Acts 2:24). Indeed, if the death of Christ is treated as the supreme demonstration of the *love* of God, his resurrection is treated as the supreme demonstration of the *power* of God. Paul, for example, prays that his converts may experience 'the immeasurable greatness of his power in us who believe, according to the working of his great might which he accomplished in Christ when he raised him from the dead' (Ephesians 1:19–20). This experience is made possible for believers in Christ because, as Paul says to the Christians in Rome, 'the Spirit of him who raised Jesus from the dead dwells in you' (Romans 8:11).

But, whatever may be said of the power at work in the actual raising of Christ from the dead, there is no doubt about the initiative in his resurrection appearances. When we read that 'he appeared' in resurrection to this, that and the next one, what is meant is that he let himself be seen by them. People are often seen without realizing that any one sees them; this never happened to the risen Christ. His resurrection appearances took a wonderful variety of forms, but no one saw or recognized him without his making sure that they did so. The two disciples on the road to Emmaus would never have noticed their sympathetic fellow traveller if he had not joined them and started a conversation with them. Even then, they would not have recognized him if he had not accepted their pressing invitation to come home with them, and made himself known to them 'in the breaking of the bread' (Luke 24:13–35).

Again, those disciples who, a short time after that, resumed their fishing on the lake of Galilee, would have paid little attention to the stranger on the beach if he had not called out to them and asked if they had caught anything (John 21:5). The idea that the disciples saw someone or something else and imagined that it was Jesus goes clean against the evidence. More often they saw their risen Lord and thought he was someone else, like Mary Magdalene 'supposing him to be the gardener' (John 20:15). He had to confront them, speak to them, show them his scars, to convince them that it was he and no one else. And certainly on the Damascus road where, as Paul says, 'last of all ... he appeared also to me' (1 Corinthians 15:8), the initiative was entirely the risen Lord's: he was the last person that Paul expected – or wished – to see or hear. The resurrection appearances constitute the first work of Christ after he left the tomb: by this work he transformed his disciples' doubt, sorrow and despair into faith, joy and hope, and made them the men and women with whom and through whom he should carry out his further work.

The shared ministry

After convincing them in this way that he was truly alive, he did not retire to a state of distant detachment, leaving them to get on as best they could with the work which he gave them to do. They were not simply to take over his work from him and carry it on in his absence. The followers of Christ do not *continue* his ministry; he *shares* his ministry with them. The initiative is still his. A summary of resurrection appearances which is included in many editions of the New Testament as an appendix to the gospel of Mark (Mark 16:9–20) concludes with the statement that the disciples 'went forth and preached everywhere, while *the Lord worked with them* and confirmed the message by the signs that attended it'.

Something to the same effect is implied in the opening words of the Acts of the Apostles. The author of this work, who had already written the gospel of Luke and dedicated it to a man named Theophilus, refers back to that earlier work in these terms: 'In the first book, O Theophilus, I have dealt with all that Jesus began to do and teach, until the day when he was taken up' (Acts 1:1–2). The implication is that Luke is now going on to deal with all that Jesus *continued* to do and teach, *since* 'the day when he was taken up'. In the Acts as much as in the gospel, the work is still the work of Christ. Only, whereas previously he carried out his work personally, in his visible presence on earth, now he carries it out from his state of exaltation, withdrawn from human sight, by his Spirit in his followers – the apostles and others. The book which we commonly call 'The Acts of the Apostles' might be called with greater accuracy, but at inconveniently greater length, 'The Acts of the Risen Christ by his Spirit in the Apostles'.

The baptism of the Spirit

The first work of Christ to be recorded in Acts after he took his leave of his followers is the bestowal on them of the Holy Spirit. We have seen how John the Baptist said that the one who was coming after him 'will baptize you with the Holy Spirit' (Mark 1:8) – a promise which was not to be fulfilled until Jesus had died. John the evangelist says that during Jesus' earthly ministry 'the Spirit had not been given, because Jesus was not yet glorified' (John 7:39) – and in the gospel of John the death of Jesus is the means of his being 'glorified'. But when Jesus appeared to his disciples after being raised from the dead, he told them that the fulfilment of the promise was now imminent: 'for John baptized with water, but before many days you shall be baptized with the Holy Spirit.' (Acts 1:5.)

So indeed it happened, for on the day of Pentecost, seven weeks after Jesus' death and resurrection, the disciples 'were all filled with the Holy Spirit' (Acts 2:4). When the crowd of spectators was amazed at the visible and audible phenomena which marked the event, Peter explained that Jesus, crucified by men but raised from the dead by God, was now 'exalted at the right hand of God, and having received from the Father the promised Holy Spirit, he has poured out this which you see and hear' (Acts 2:33).

The baptism of the Spirit, or baptism with the Spirit, is thus the work of the risen Christ. By this act he brought his church into being. The church – the people of God in New Testament times – is continuous with the people of God in Old Testament times; but on that day of Pentecost it experienced a new beginning, a spiritual rebirth. Jesus is the representative of the people of God in Old and New Testament times alike; when he descended into death and rose again, the people of God symbolically died and rose with him. 'The Spirit of him who raised Jesus from the dead' now came to dwell in his followers and made them a new community – the community of which Jesus had said, 'I will build my church, and the gates of Hades [the powers of death] shall not prevail against it' (Matthew 16:18). Whereas the people of God in Old Testament times had been almost entirely confined to members of one nation, the reborn people of God, endowed by Jesus with his Spirit, speedily came to embrace men and women of many nations.

There is only one place in the whole New Testament outside the gospels and Acts – in other words, there is only one place apart from those which record or echo the promise of John the Baptist – where the baptism of the Spirit is mentioned. That is in 1 Corinthians 12:13, where Paul reminds his converts in Corinth that 'in one Spirit we were all baptized into one body'; and here the meaning of the Pentecostal event is made plain. It is the risen Christ who baptizes his people – *all* his people – 'in one Spirit', and by this baptism they are incorporated 'into one body'. The 'body', or the 'body of Christ', is Paul's distinctive term for the new, Spirit-indwelt community. The baptism of the Spirit is an expression which is often used loosely; it is helpful to mark what its New Testment meaning is, and to bear in mind that it is a very important work of Christ.

The powerful name

It became evident that Christ, though no longer visible on earth, was still powerfully at work through his disciples when the witness of Peter and his companions on the day of Pentecost brought three thousand people into the new community. Jesus' followers during his earthly ministry could be numbered in hundreds, at most; from now on they were to be reckoned in thousands and, after a few years, in tens of thousands. The disciples claimed no credit for themselves: this rapid increase in the number of believers in Jesus was due to his power or, as they liked to say, his name. Those authorities in Jerusalem who felt that they could breathe more easily when Jesus was safely buried were now greatly disturbed. They did not believe that he had risen from the dead, but they could see that in death (as they thought) he was winning more followers than ever he had won in his life.

It was not only in the apostles' preaching that his power was manifested; they began to do, in his name, the same kind of mighty works as he himself had done when he was with them. One incident which the chief priests took very seriously was the healing of a man, a cripple from birth, who used to sit begging at one of the gates within the temple precincts. The healing of a cripple was, of course, no crime; but this healing act took place at a time when a large crowd had gathered in the temple courts, and it made a tremendous impression on them. Moreover, it was done explicitly 'in the name of Jesus Christ of Nazareth', and the implications of this fact were brought home to the crowd of spectators as Peter addressed them in Solomon's colonnade, at the east end of the outer court. The spectacle of the man whose lameness had been cured, 'walking and leaping and praising God' (Acts 3:8), was seen by many as an eloquent confirmation of the apostles' message: it showed that Jesus really was alive and active among them.

The apostles were arrested for causing a disturbance, or for hindering free movement by collecting a crowd within the temple area; but when they were brought before the court next day no action could be taken against them. They maintained that the cripple had been healed 'by the name of Jesus Christ of Nazareth ... whom God raised from the dead' (Acts 4:10). It was clear that the man had been cured, and there could be no doubt about the genuineness of the cure. Everyone who had occasion to visit the temple knew him; he had sat there begging for years. The court acknowledged that a remarkable and undeniable 'sign' had been performed. All they could do was to forbid the disciples to mention the name of Jesus in public; but this order the disciples ignored. So the power of the name of Jesus spread, not in Jerusalem only, but among Samaritans and Gentiles too.

When Christians began to preach the gospel in more distant lands, the same mighty works accompanied them as had been seen in the early days in Jerusalem. Thus we are told that when Paul and Barnabas visited Iconium (the modern Konya in Turkey) and 'spoke out boldly for the Lord', Jesus 'bore witness that this was indeed the message of his grace by enabling them to perform signs and wonders' (Acts 14:3). Later, in Ephesus, 'the name of the Lord Jesus was extolled' as his powerful presence was made public in the ministry of Paul and his helpers (Acts 19:17). And so the story unfolds until, at the end of Acts, Paul is brought to Rome and bears his witness in the imperial city itself, without let or hindrance.

This is not simply the way in which Luke tells his story in Acts. When Paul himself describes what *we* might call his achievements, he speaks of 'what *Christ* has accomplished through me to win obedience from the Gentiles, by word and deed, by the power of signs and wonders, by the power of the Holy Spirit' (Romans 15:18–19).

It is plain, then, that the same kind of miracles as had marked the ministry of Jesus continued to mark the ministry of his disciples throughout the apostolic age. The disciples did not see anything extraordinary about this: they had been led to expect that Jesus would still be with them, and these things were evidence that he actually was with them. The miracles were so well known that the disciples could point to them as evidence of the continuing presence and power of Jesus. It was not simply the fact that they were miracles that was important: it was their nature. Not only were they miracles of the same kind as Jesus had done; just as Jesus' works of mercy and power had illustrated and confirmed the main themes of his preaching, so the 'signs and wonders' performed by the apostles illustrated and confirmed their witness to him.

A continuing story

The Acts of the Apostles does not end haphazardly; Luke has achieved his purpose when he brings Paul to Rome and leaves him preaching the gospel there. Yet there is a sense in which the Acts of the Apostles is an unfinished book; at least the story which it begins to tell is an unfinished story. Luke tells how the gospel spread within one generation; the same gospel has been spreading generation by generation ever since:

> Nor shall thy spreading gospel rest
> > Till through the world thy truth has run;
> Till Christ has all the nations blest
> > That see the light or feel the sun.

Towards the end of the nineteenth century a book was published with the title *The New Acts of the Apostles*, by Dr A. T. Pierson. This was a survey of Christian missions from the thirteenth century to the author's own day. He drew many parallels between the apostolic age and more recent times, acknowledging that 'the New Acts of the Apostles is, like the Old, an unfinished book'. But he emphasized that the secret of the new Acts, as of the old, was the abiding activity of Christ with and through his messengers. There would be further advances, further conquests, 'until God's chosen heralds leave no Regions Beyond unpenetrated, and no creature unreached'. But, he emphasized in the last sentence of the book, 'all this depends on the manifested Presence of the Redeemer, in the power of that Holy Spirit, whose holy ministries made luminous with glory the Acts of the Apostles!'

Of course, to talk about apostles in this more recent context is to use the word in a wider sense than Luke intended. But in this wider sense 'apostle' means 'messenger' or 'agent'. The original apostles were Jesus' special agents, directly chosen and commissioned by him; but Jesus has had many agents in all succeeding ages. Only, there is this difference between his agents and other people's: he accompanies his agents. He does not energize them by remote control; he is present with them by his Spirit. They work for him, but he works in them. He does not set the work going, and then leave it to carry on by its own momentum; he keeps it going.

4

CHRIST
OUR RIGHTEOUSNESS

Some of the most important teaching about the work of Christ
in the New Testament is found in the letters of Paul. Paul made
a notable contribution to the New Testament: out of its twenty-
seven documents, thirteen bear his name as their author.

'What the law could not do'

Paul's principal claim on our attention lies in the fact that it
was he, far more than any other person, who introduced
Christianity to the Gentiles – that is to say, to people who were
not Jews by birth. Jesus himself belonged to the Jewish nation,
and so did all his apostles and the others whom he chose to
be his disciples or pupils. It is sometimes said that the movement which he started would have remained a party within the
Jewish nation if it had not been for Paul. This is probably an
exaggeration, for Paul was not the only one in New Testament
times who preached the gospel to Gentiles, but he was specially
selected and commissioned by the risen Christ to be his apostle
to the Gentiles.

This might seem surprising, for Paul in his earlier days was
a more dyed-in-the-wool Jew than any of the original apostles
of Jesus. Unlike them, he was trained to be a doctor of the
law of Israel, and he devoted himself wholeheartedly to the
study, practice and defence of that law. Far from being well-
disposed to Jesus and the gospel in his earlier days, he was
convinced, as he put it himself, that he 'ought to do many

things in opposing the name of Jesus of Nazareth' (Acts 26:9). His religion was based on the works of the law, not on the work of Christ. He thought that the gospel presented a mortal threat to the law and the traditions which he held so dear, and he would gladly have exterminated the followers of Jesus. We first meet Paul not as an apostle but as a persecutor.

What happened, then, to bring about such a change in him? According to his own account and the account given by Luke in the Acts of the Apostles, he was confronted, arrested, stopped dead in his tracks by the risen Christ when he was furiously engaged in hot pursuit and persecution of Christians. 'I saw Jesus our Lord,' he says; 'God was pleased to reveal his Son to me' (1 Corinthians 9:1; Galatians 1:16). In one lightning flash he learned two things: one, that Jesus of Nazareth was indeed Messiah, Lord, and Son of God, as his followers claimed him to be; and the other, that he himself was being conscripted there and then by this Lord to be his servant, to carry the knowledge of him to the Gentile world.

Paul's conversion on the Damascus road compelled him to make a radical re-assessment of the person of Jesus. It also compelled him to think seriously about the work of Jesus.

Paul had been sure that Jesus could not be the Messiah, in spite of his followers' claims. His reasoning was simple and, as he thought, foolproof. The Messiah was, almost by definition, a person on whom the blessing of God rested in a unique degree: 'all nations shall call him blessed,' said one of the messianic psalms (Psalm 72:17). But in dying on a cross, Jesus died under the *curse* of God. There could be no doubt about that: the law said plainly in Deuteronomy 21:23, 'a hanged man is accursed by God'. Whether Jesus was crucified justly or unjustly was beside the point; the bare fact that he was crucified at all brought him into the category of those described as 'accursed by God'.

But when Paul's experience on the Damascus road assured him that Jesus was indeed the Messiah, it did not remove the undoubted fact that Jesus had died on a cross – had died, therefore, under the curse of God. How could this have happened?

Paul found the solution to this problem in the Old Testament law itself. In the very book which pronounced the divine curse on anyone who was hanged – Deuteronomy – he recalled another passage which pronounced the divine curse in a different context. This was the last and most comprehensive of a series of twelve curses pronounced on people who broke the law of God, and it ran: 'Cursed be everyone who does not abide by all things written in the book of the law, and do them.' (Deuteronomy 27:26.)

Paul had been aware of this comprehensive curse ever since he began to study the law, and he took it very seriously. He knew some teachers of the law who held that God would be satisfied with any one who, with good intentions, managed to keep the law more often than he broke it. Anyone who scored more than half marks, so to speak, would pass. But Paul could not accept this. The law, as he understood it, demanded total obedience; someone who scored ninety-nine per cent would incur the curse of the law for the one per cent which he broke.

It was possible, by infinite painstaking, for a person to achieve – or to believe he had achieved – 100 per cent. Of course he could not be sure until the day of judgement, but we remember one man who heard Jesus recite the commandments and assured him that he had kept them all since his childhood. Jesus did not question his claim, but pointed out that one could go farther than keeping the letter of the commandments. Paul too in his youth attained full marks (as he reckoned) in his endeavour to attain the standard of righteousness involved in keeping the law, but on the Damascus road he learned that he had been persisting in a very sinful course. Without realizing it, he had been persecuting the followers of the Messiah, and in principle persecuting the Messiah himself. But all the time he thought he was serving God and defending his law! The law to which he was so devoted could not prevent him from committing this sin of sins; indeed, it was the law that made him commit it. He had tried with all his might to avoid the curse which the law pronounced on the law-breaker, but he had incurred that curse more thoroughly than anyone else! Was there any hope for him, and for other law-breakers? If even he had failed to avoid the curse, what about those who had not pursued the way of legal righteousness so conscientiously as he had done?

Yes, there was hope for him and for all others – but not a hope which the law held out. The law indeed promised life to those who kept it perfectly, but no one had kept it perfectly, not even Paul himself. No one had kept it perfectly, with one exception; and that was Jesus. He alone lived a life of complete obedience to God; he alone was not liable to 'the curse of the law'. But Jesus voluntarily submitted to the divine curse when he suffered death on the cross, in order that the curse which others had incurred by disobedience to God might be transferred to him, and others might be released from it.

This, then, was the solution which Paul found in the Old Testament scriptures. He says (Galatians 3:13):

> Christ has redeemed us from the curse of the law by becoming a curse for us, in accordance with the scripture which says, 'Cursed is every one who hangs on a gibbet'.

In Paul's study of the interpretation of the Bible, one of the principles he had learned was that, where two texts had an important term in common, one of them was likely to shed light on the other. Here were two texts in Deuteronomy which shared the term 'cursed'; and if one of them presented a difficulty, the other might point the way to the removal of the difficulty. The text pronouncing a curse on anyone who was hanged (or crucified) certainly presented a colossal difficulty, when it was considered that this was the way in which Christ died. But for Paul the text pronouncing a curse on the law-breaker pointed the way to the removal of this difficulty: Christ, by dying on a cross, accepted the curse to which all but himself were exposed because of their failure to keep the law.

How could this vicarious curse-bearing of Christ be appropriated by its intended beneficiaries? By faith. Anyone who – in theory, at least – gained life through keeping the law gained it as the reward which his achievement had earned. It was a matter of work and merit. But anyone who had failed to keep the law – and that meant everyone – could make no claim to such a reward. The law which pronounced blessing and life on those who obeyed it pronounced cursing and death on those who disobeyed it. If those who disobeyed it were nevertheless admitted to blessing and life, it could not be on the score of merit, but on the ground of God's grace. This is precisely what the gospel proclaims. God's grace had provided release from the curse and the assurance of life through the cross of Christ, and what had been provided by God's grace could be appropriated only by grateful trust in him.

Long before the law was given, Paul adds, Abraham, the spiritual father of all who have faith in God, 'believed God, and it was reckoned to him for righteousness' (Romans 4:3). Abraham received unprecedented blessing from God, with the promise that through him and his offspring blessing would come to all the nations. This promise was fulfilled in the gospel, and the offspring of Abraham through whom blessing was to come to all nations was pre-eminently Christ. Where the law was concerned, Jews had an advantage over all other nations, for it was to them that the law was given. But where divine grace and the response of faith were concerned, Jews and Gentiles were on an equal footing. The purpose of Christ's endurance of death on a cross was that the blessing promised to Abraham might be extended to all nations – Gentiles as well as Jews – 'that we might receive the promise of the Spirit through faith' (Galatians 3:14). The Spirit whom believers in Christ have received is the Spirit of freedom: instead of conforming their lives to a code of laws – instead of 'working to rule', we might say – they allow the Spirit to reproduce his 'fruit', the sum-total of Christian graces, in their lives from within. This is the freedom for which Christ set them free: to retreat from it would be to 'submit again to a yoke of slavery' (Galatians 5:1).

Paul's gospel

In expounding the work of Christ in these terms, Paul obviously reflects his own experience. This is the logical implication of what happened to him on the Damascus road. But, while he had his own way of setting forth the gospel, the gospel which he set forth was not peculiar to himself; it was shared with those who had been apostles before him.

There is one place where Paul has occasion to summarize the basic facts of the gospel. His converts in Corinth needed to be reminded of the message which he brought when first he visited their city, and he reminds them of it in these terms:

> I delivered to you as of first importance what I myself had received – namely, (a) that Christ died for our sins in accordance with the scriptures; (b) that he was buried; (c) that he was raised again on the third day in accordance with the scriptures; (d) that he appeared to Cephas [Peter], then to the twelve, then to more than five hundred of our brothers on one and the same occasion (most of them are still alive, though some have fallen asleep); then he appeared to James [his brother], then to all the apostles.

This was all part of the general testimony of the apostles and their associates; Paul adds his own contribution: 'Last of all he appeared to me also.' Then, after a brief digression in which he emphasizes how unworthy he was to see the risen Christ and be commissioned by him as an apostle, he concludes the summary by saying, 'Whether then it was I or they [the other apostles and their associates], this is what we preach; this is what you believed.' (1 Corinthians 15:3–11.)

The particular matter on which Paul lays special emphasis in this summary is the reality of the resurrection of Christ, but it is worth looking at the terms in which he mentions (almost in passing) the death of Christ. 'Christ died for our sins,' he says, 'in accordance with the scriptures.' Three points are made here: first, the person who died was Christ – that is, the Messiah, the Lord's anointed; secondly, he died for his people's sins; thirdly, he died in accordance with the scriptures.

Before his conversion, Paul would not have spoken of Jesus as 'Christ'; to do so would have been to concede the very claim that he then believed to be impossible and blasphemous – that the crucified one could be the Lord's anointed. But after his conversion he came to refer to Jesus habitually as 'Christ' almost as if it were his personal name.

When he says 'Christ died for our sins', he says something which was certainly integral to the gospel as he himself preached it. The natural inference to draw from his saying so here is that the other apostles also taught that Christ died for his people's sins. This has sometimes been questioned, but two things should be said. First, Paul is by no means the only New Testament writer to say that Jesus' death was endured in some sense for his people's sins. Indeed, as we have seen, Jesus implied as much himself when he said that the Son of Man came to give his life a ransom for many, especially if the reference in these words is to Isaiah's suffering Servant. Secondly, when Christ is said to have died 'in accordance with the scriptures', the passage which tells how the suffering Servant 'makes himself an offering for sin' (Isaiah 53:10) is most probably one of the scriptures meant. If that is so, the scriptures which were fulfilled in Jesus' death were fulfilled more specifically in his death *for sin*.

What Paul himself meant by Jesus' dying for his people's sins is seen more clearly in other places in his correspondence.

In 2 Corinthians 5:18 he speaks of the gospel with which he and his fellow apostles had been entrusted as 'the ministry of reconciliation'. He goes on to say, in explanation of this, that 'God was in Christ reconciling the world to himself' (verse 19). The world of mankind, by its disobedience to God, was alienated from him, hostile to him, but in Christ God took the initiative in reconciling sinful humanity to himself. An Old Testament prophet had assured his contemporaries that God's plans for them were plans 'of peace, and not of evil' (Jeremiah 29:11). The same assurance is expressed in the gospel. Paul depicts the preachers of the gospel as 'ambassadors for Christ', proclaiming the divine amnesty, urging men and women to accept his terms of peace (2 Corinthians 5:20–21):

We beseech you on behalf of Christ, be reconciled to God. For

our sake he made him to be sin who knew no sin, so that in him
we might become the righteousness of God.

To use the words of an anonymous second-century Christian,
here is a 'sweet exchange' indeed. Christ, who was without sin,
was 'made sin' for sinners, in order that sinners might be made
not merely righteous, but righteousness itself – God's own
righteousness – in him. He voluntarily took our sin and guilt
on himself, so that we in exchange might be invested with
his righteousness and become, in him, as acceptable to God
as he himself is. This is what is meant when people speak about
'justification by faith'.

Getting right with God

In a later letter, written to the Christians in Rome, Paul spells
out more fully what this involves. After showing that Jews and
Gentiles alike have failed to measure up to the requirements
of God's law, and must abandon all hope of *earning* his acceptance, he speaks of the new way to get right with God which
is opened up in the gospel, thanks to the liberating work of
Christ.

To set forth this liberating work, Paul has recourse to a variety
of analogies from human life. Each analogy makes its contribution to this end; none by itself could exhaust the reality.
Speaking of God's new way of setting men and women right
(putting them 'in the clear', we might say), Paul says that we
are 'justified freely by his grace, through the redemption that
is in Christ Jesus, whom God has set forth as an atonement,
by means of his blood, to be received by faith' (Romans
3:24–25).

Here, to take them in the reverse order, we have the analogy
of the temple ('atonement'), of the slave market ('redemption')
and of the law court ('being justified').

As for the analogy of the temple, Christ is described as the
one who has made atonement for his people's sins. This language
reminds us of the sacrificial system laid down in Old Testament
times, which included the institution of the sin-offering. There

was one special sin-offering associated with the annual day of atonement in Israel, when an animal was sacrificed in the precincts of the temple. Its blood was carried by the high priest into the holy of holies, the inner compartment of the temple, where the ark of the covenant stood. This was surmounted by what was called the 'mercy seat', the throne of the invisible presence of God. It was called the 'mercy seat' or 'throne of grace' because it was there that atonement was effected, there that God, through the high priest, gave his people the assurance of his pardoning grace.

Some scholars think that the word which Paul uses for 'atonement' actually means 'mercy seat'. If that is what Paul had in mind, then perhaps he meant that, unlike the original place of atonement, concealed in the holy of holies behind a heavy curtain, Christ was brought out to accomplish his atoning work before the public gaze, just as he is now publicly proclaimed as a sin-atoning sacrifice.

However, Paul need not have been thinking of the actual mercy seat. He may mean, more generally, that Jesus is presented in the gospel as the one who atones for his people's sins, just as later in the same letter he says that God sent his own Son as an offering 'for sin' (Romans 8:3). The thought in any case is that of a sacrifice: that is the sense of the phrase 'by means of his blood', which the New English Bible translates 'by his sacrificial death' (Romans 3:25). Jesus, that is to say, offered his life up to God in the hour of suffering and death as an atonement for the sins of the human race. The idea of presenting one's life to God as an atonement for others was not new in Israel. The martyrs who died for their faith in the days of the Maccabean revolt, nearly two centuries before the death of Christ, offered up their lives as an atonement for their fellow Israelites. But in the death of Christ we see the representative man, the one who was free from sin, yielding his life to God for the blessing of mankind in general.

In the analogy of the slave market sin is practically personified as a grim slave-owner who keeps the souls of men and women in bondage, forcing them to do things of which their better

selves disapprove. They are quite unable by their own strength
to redeem themselves from this power, but what they cannot
do for themselves has been done for them by another. They
can be set free from the spiritual slavery in which they are held
by 'the redemption which is in Christ Jesus' (Romans 3:24)
– or, to quote the New English Bible again, God's 'act of
liberation in the person of Christ Jesus'. This analogy cannot
be pressed too far. Christ does indeed pay the price of liberation,
that price being his own life. But he does not pay it to the slave-
owner; this slave-owner is a usurper, who exercises power over
the lives of human beings without any right to do so. If the
price is paid to anyone, it is paid to God, although this is not
explicitly said here by Paul.

The analogy which came most naturally to Paul was that of
the law-court. This was because Paul in his earlier life had
regarded true religion as a matter of obeying the law of God.
In those days he evidently hoped that, by perseverance in
obeying God's law, he might at last be pronounced righteous
by God when he stood before his judgement seat. But in the
new way of 'righteousness' revealed in the gospel the procedure
is reversed. God pronounces people righteous at the beginning
of the course, not at the end of it. If, however, he pronounces
them righteous at the beginning of the course, it cannot be on
the basis of deeds which they have not yet done. It can be only
on the basis of his free grace, and can be received only by glad
and open-hearted faith.

Paul found it much more satisfying to know himself 'justified
freely' by God's grace than to hope that he might be justified
– pronounced righteous – on the great day by his record of
keeping the law. It is easy to sympathize with him. If we hope
to earn God's favourable verdict because of what we have done,
we can never be sure that we have made the grade. Our record
is in any case much less satisfactory than Paul at one time
thought his was. And even if we always do the best we can
(which, in common honesty, we don't), how can we be certain
that our best will pass muster with God? But if God in sheer
grace assures me in advance that he has accepted me, forgiven

me, set me right with himself, and I thankfully embrace his
assurance, then I can go on to do his will in the power of·the
new life which he gives without always worrying whether I am
doing it adequately· or not. In fact, to the end of the chapter
I shall be an unprofitable servant, but I know whom I have
believed:

> He owns me for his child;
> I can no longer fear.

5

CHRIST
THE CONQUEROR

We may have dealt with the most important aspect of Paul's teaching about the work of Christ, but we have not exhausted what he has to say on the subject.

The powers of evil

Let us go back to his letter to the Galatians – perhaps the first of his letters that has been preserved. He begins it by wishing his readers grace and peace 'from God the Father and our Lord Jesus Christ, who gave himself for our sins to deliver us from the present evil age'. These words will repay careful examination.

The 'present age' is called evil because it was dominated by the forces of wickedness. This was not a view peculiar to Paul; we find it paralleled in the religious community of Qumran, north-west of the Dead Sea, a century and more before Paul's time. The pious Jews of Qumran (whose beliefs are set down in the documents popularly called the Dead Sea Scrolls) referred to the age in which they were living as the 'epoch of wickedness'. They believed it would soon be brought to an end by the direct intervention of God, and they believed that their community had been called into being to make preparation for his intervention. For Paul, God had already intervened by sending his Son into the world. Until Christ came there was no effective deliverance from the forces of wickedness, but he came to bring about this deliverance. The deliverance was not completed immediately; the 'present age' did not come to an end all at once; but the work of Christ inaugurated a new age, which is destined to go on increasing, while the 'present age' will go on diminishing until it disappears and is altogether superseded by the new age. Meanwhile, the two ages overlap – the 'evil age' which dominated the situation before Christ came and the age of goodness and truth which he introduced. But in this overlapping period, those whom he has delivered can experience the powerful forces of the new age, operating under the control of his Spirit, so that they can resist and overcome the evil forces of the old age.

Sometimes these forces are pictured by Paul in personal terms. Indeed, we have seen how Jesus himself had set the example in this matter. When he was actively liberating the minds of those who were possessed by 'evil spirits', he compared them to the captives of a strong man who held his fortress against all comers until a stronger man than he laid siege to it. 'No one can enter a strong man's house and plunder his goods, unless he first binds the strong man; then indeed he may plunder his house.' (Mark 3:27.) The strong man was the prince of the demons, but the stronger man was Jesus, coming in the power of the kingdom of God and forcing the strong man to relinquish his prey.

In one place Paul speaks about the wisdom of God which is enshrined in the gospel, wisdom concealed from those who are spiritually blind but revealed by the Spirit to men and women of faith. 'None of the rulers of this age understood this,' he says; 'for if they had, they would not have crucified the Lord of glory.' (1 Corinthians 2:8.) He may be referring to such 'rulers' as Caiaphas the high priest, Herod Antipas the ruler of Galilee and Pontius Pilate the governor of Judaea, who shared the responsibility for the condemnation and death of Jesus and certainly had no inkling of the new power that was about to be let loose in the world as a result. But more probably he is referring to spiritual forces operating behind those human rulers, using the latter as their 'front-men'. These are the forces of which he elsewhere speaks as 'principalities and powers'. This phrase has passed into the language of our hymns:

Principalities and powers,
Mustering their unseen array,
Wait for thine unguarded hours;
Watch and pray.

The reigning Christ

At a later point in 1 Corinthians, Paul says that the resurrection
of Christ (which is past) is the guarantee of the resurrection of
his people (which is future). His resurrection is like the first
ripe sheaf of grain which was dedicated to God in the temple;
their resurrection is the full harvest of which the first ripe sheaf
was the promise. 'But each in his own order,' he says: 'Christ
the first fruits, then at his coming those who belong to Christ.
Then comes the end, when he delivers the kingdom to God
the Father after destroying every principality and power, every
force opposed to him.' That is what is meant when it is said
in Psalm 110:1 that all his enemies are to be made his footstool.
Until then, he must continue to reign. 'The last enemy to be
destroyed is death.' (1 Corinthians 15:23–26.)

This means that between his resurrection and his coming
in glory Christ is reigning from his place of enthronement –
'at God's right hand', as the vivid expression of Psalm 110:1
puts it (see page 73). (The people of New Testament times knew
as well as we do that God has no literal right hand; the expression denoted supremacy over the universe.) While he is
reigning, all the hostile forces in the universe are being pro-
gressively put down by him. This is what is meant by words
which we sometimes sing:

He sits at God's right hand
Till all his foes submit,
And bow at his command
And fall beneath his feet.

The most powerful of these hostile forces is death itself, but
at last even death will be abolished. The abolition of death is
another way of describing the resurrection of those who belong

to Christ, which will take place at his second coming.

Several years ago a European scholar, Oscar Cullmann, compared this aspect of the work of Christ to the progress of a great war – in this case, the war between good and evil. In a great war there is often one battle which decides the outcome of the war. After this decisive battle has been fought and won, there is little doubt which side will be victorious, but no one can say how long the war will yet go on. D-day, the day of the decisive battle, is past, but V-day, the day of the victory celebrations, lies in the future.

In the long drawn-out war between good and evil, the decisive battle was fought and won by Christ in his death and resurrection. If death is personified as a hostile force, then death proved incapable of keeping Christ in his prison-house. Christ forced his way out, and in doing so he disabled death. Death is still active, but for those who belong to Christ death has lost its terror, because they know that their Master has conquered death and will one day deal death its death-blow. When that day dawns they will share their Master's resurrection and join in the victory celebrations. The war will be over for good and all.

There are other hostile forces in the universe which continue to enslave the minds of those men and women who submit to them, but Christ is their conqueror too. They have no power over those whom Christ has delivered from their influence; to them they have become 'weak and beggarly elements' (to use another of Paul's expressions), no longer able to assert control.

If the decisive battle determined the outcome of the war, it could be said that those forces whose defeat was then sealed were in principle defeated when the decisive battle was fought. Thus, while Paul speaks of death in 1 Corinthians 15:26 as the last enemy which is to be abolished, we read in 2 Timothy 1:10 that Christ has already 'abolished death and brought life and immortality to light through the gospel'.

The rout of demonic forces

But there is one place in particular where Paul gives a striking word-picture of the decisive battle and the overthrow of hostile forces. In Colossians 2:13–15 he speaks of the acknowledged sins of the people of Christ as a 'bond' or IOU which they had signed and which was being held over them threateningly by blackmailing 'principalities and powers' to compel them to do their bidding. But Christ, says Paul,

> cancelled the bond which stood against us with its legal demands; he set it aside, nailing it to the cross. He disarmed the principalities and powers and made a public example of them, triumphing over them by means of the cross.

Nowhere has Paul given us a more dramatic presentation of the work of Christ than this. Our sins, he says, represented a mountain of bankruptcy which could not be disowned and could not be discharged. But Christ has wiped the slate clean and given us a fresh start. He took that signed confession of indebtedness which stood as a damning indictment against us, and cancelled it by his death. One might actually say that he took the document and nailed it to his cross as an act of sovereign defiance in face of those blackmailing powers which were holding it over us as a threat.

Perhaps he means that figuratively Jesus did with this 'bond' what was literally done with his own accusation. His accusation, nailed in mockery above his head, read 'The King of the Jews'. But what was intended in mockery has ever since been recognized by many as the proclamation of the royal state of the kingliest King of all. So, figuratively, the 'bond' which was our certificate of enslavement has been taken by him and turned into our diploma of release. Krishna Pal, William Carey's first convert when he went to India as a missionary at the end of the eighteenth century, caught something of the spirit of Paul's metaphor when he wrote:

> Jesus for thee a body takes,
> Thy guilt assumes, thy fetters breaks,
> Discharging all thy dreadful debt –
> And canst thou then such love forget?

Christ by his death on the cross releases his people not only from the guilt of sin but also from its dominion over them. Not only, says Paul, has he cancelled our debt but he has conquered those spiritual enemies whose possession of the 'bond' kept us in their grip. Those same spiritual enemies thought they had him in their grasp when he was fastened to the cross, that instrument of disgrace and death. But he turned it into the instrument of their defeat and captivity. As he was suspended there, bound hand and foot to the wood in apparent weakness, they thought they had him at their mercy, and flung themselves on him with malicious intent. If, in the pain of death, he had cursed his enemies or blasphemed God, they would have won. But as he prayed for the forgiveness of his executioners and committed his spirit to God, it was evident that they were defeated. Or, as Paul's bold picture expresses it, he did not endure their assault unresistingly. Far from it; in the spirit-realm he grappled with them and mastered them, stripped them of all their armour, and (so to speak) held them aloft in his mighty hands, displaying to the universe their helplessness and his own unconquered strength. Now they are dethroned and disabled, and (by a change of the figure) the cross has become the triumphal chariot in which the victor rides, driving them as captives before him, unwilling confessors that in him they have met their match – and more.

This picture of the victory of Christ corresponded to something real in the experience of first-century Christians. They knew that Christ had come into their lives and set them free from forces that had enslaved them. Perhaps they envisaged those forces as demons and thought of them as having personally received their death-blow from the crucified and risen Christ; but, one way or the other, they recognized that they themselves enjoyed the benefits of Christ's victory.

Most men and women in the western world today may not think in such personal terms of the forces that hold the minds of individuals and communities in bondage. But they are so acutely aware of the power and malignity of those forces that they sometimes describe them as 'demonic'. Many of them feel that they are little better than puppets in the hands of a blind and unfriendly fate. Others are concerned about being involved in movements and situations against which their moral sense revolts, but they cannot see any effective way of resistance. The letter to the Colossians has a powerful message for such a time as this. The crucified and risen Christ is Lord of all: all the forces in the universe are subject to him. Therefore those who are united to him by faith share in his victory. Through his power they too can conquer the forces of evil and enjoy perfect freedom. They can know, as Paul did, that neither principalities nor powers nor any other force in the universe can 'separate us from the love of God in Christ Jesus our Lord' (Romans 8:39).

His people's present helper

That, then, is one thing which the risen Christ is doing for his people here and now – enabling them to enjoy freedom from the hostile forces which he has conquered. Another way of putting it comes in what may be a quotation from a confession of faith current among Christians of the first generation. In answer to the challenge, 'Who will bring any charge against God's chosen people?', Paul says (Romans 8:33–34):

> It is God who justifies; who is to condemn? Is it Christ Jesus, who died, yes, who was raised from the dead, who is at the right hand of God, who indeed intercedes for us?

If he is picturing the divine law-court, he seems to say that Christ, raised by God to the highest place that heaven affords, is his people's counsel for the defence, not their prosecutor.

John Bunyan tells us in *Grace Abounding* how he once received great comfort, in a time of inward distress, from the text where believers in God are said to be 'justified freely by his grace, through the redemption that is in Christ Jesus' (see page 58). It was, he says, as though God were addressing him thus:

> Sinner, thou thinkest that because of thy sins and infirmities I cannot save thy soul, but behold my Son is by me, and upon him

I look, and not on thee, and will deal with thee according as I am pleased with him.

This confidence is included in Paul's statement that the risen Christ 'intercedes' for his people. But more than this is included. If Christ 'intercedes' for them, he is their representative with God. And this representative is so completely acceptable to God that he can draw at will on the limitless resources of divine grace and power and make them freely available to his people. In trial and temptation, in sorrow or danger, or when they are faced with responsibilities too great for their natural strength, his people receive from him for the asking the spiritual resources they need.

Paul proved this in his own experience. When, not long after the beginning of his apostolic career, he was attacked by an unpleasant and humiliating complaint which he thought would put an end to his usefulness in the service of Christ, he prayed to have it removed. It was not removed; he had to live with it from then on. But his prayer was answered all the same. If the complaint was not taken away, he was given additional strength to endure it – but to see how it could be overruled so as to become an asset to his apostolic service, not a hindrance. The risen Lord's answer to his prayer took the form of words: 'My grace is sufficient for you, for my power is made perfect in weakness.' (2 Corinthians 12:9.)

Much of what Paul says of the present work of Christ, however, is bound up with what he says of the ministry of the Spirit. The Spirit conveys what Christ bestows. It is remarkable in how many interchangeable ways Paul speaks of the present work of Christ and the work of the Spirit. If Christ intercedes for us, so does the Spirit; the freedom for which Christ has set us free is the freedom of the Spirit; we are 'in Christ' and 'in the Spirit'; Christ is in us and so is the Spirit. The present work of Christ, then, so far as Paul's account is concerned, cannot be dissociated from the present work of the Spirit (which is treated in detail in a companion volume in this series).

The present work of the Spirit, moreover, is preparing us

for the future work of Christ. The indwelling Spirit is the pledge here and now of coming immortality. The saving work of Christ reaches its climax in the final resurrection of his people, when 'the mortal puts on immortality' and 'death is swallowed up in victory' (1 Corinthians 15:54). Something more will be said about this when we look in greater detail at 'the future work of Christ' (page 123). But here and now his people may anticipate the victory celebrations of the end-time and make Paul's words their own: 'thanks be to God, who gives us the victory through our Lord Jesus Christ.' (1 Corinthians 15:57.)

6

PRIEST AND SACRIFICE

Paul, as we have seen (page 68), speaks of Christ as the one who at present 'intercedes for us'. He does not enlarge on this – he is probably quoting part of an early confession of faith – and we might wonder what form this intercession takes. It might help us to recall the words of encouragement spoken to Peter when Jesus exposed the hollowness of his self-confidence and foretold how he would deny him. 'I have prayed for you,' said Jesus, 'that your faith may not fail.' (Luke 22:32.) In consequence, Peter's own faith would be restored and he would be able to strengthen the faith of others. So we might say that what Jesus did for Peter on earth he continues to do for all his people in his present state of exaltation. That would be the truth, but it would not be the whole truth.

Our great high priest

In many religious systems there is a functionary whose special responsibility it is to represent his fellows before God and, when necessary, to intercede for them with God. He is commonly called a priest. This might seem to be a suitable title to apply to Jesus in relation to his people. But the actual title, as distinct from the truth it expresses, is given to him in only one book of the New Testament – the anonymous letter to the Hebrews. (If we call it an 'anonymous' letter we mean that *we* are not sure who wrote it; the people for whom it was originally intended were not in any doubt about its authorship.)

The people for whom this letter was composed appear to

have been Jewish Christians; that is to say, they had been born and brought up as Jews, but had learned to put their faith in Jesus as Messiah. In the first fine careless rapture of their conversion they were quite prepared to find the Christian way a hard way. When they were persecuted for their faith, when their homes were looted and they themselves imprisoned, they rejoiced that they were counted worthy to suffer for the name of Christ. But the years went by; the way became no easier; their enthusiasm waned and their hope became less bright. The venerable form of worship which they had abandoned for Christ's sake showed no sign of disappearing. The temple still stood in Jerusalem; it had not been thrown down as Christ had said it would. The priests continued to offer up sacrifices there as their predecessors had done. Throughout the Roman Empire the Jews continued to enjoy the protection of the law as an authorized association. Some of these Jewish Christians began to wonder if they had not been too hasty in leaving all that for the uncertainty of Christian life. Might it not be wise to go back to the Jewish fold, or at least to keep one foot in either camp – one in the synagogue and one in the church – until they saw the situation more clearly?

It was while they were in this mood of uncertainty that they received this letter from a friend who had known them for many years. If it had been possible for him to visit them and talk to them, he would have done so. But as this was not possible for the time being, he did the next best thing and sent them in writing what he would have preferred to say face to face. (I refer to the author as 'he' because it would be awkward to say 'he or she' all the time. It has been seriously proposed that the letter was composed by Priscilla, even if it was issued under her husband's name. But, I repeat, we do not know who wrote it.)

How then, was the readers' problem to be dealt with? They had to be convinced of the finality and perfection of the gospel, and the writer undertook so to convince them by giving them such a presentation of the person and work of Christ that they could never dream of giving up their faith in him for anything else. Christ, he assures them, is the eternal Son of God through whom he brought the world of space and time into being, and by whose enabling word the universe is sustained moment by moment. Christ is God's ultimate and complete self-revelation to the human race: all earlier forms of divine self-revelation were preparatory and piecemeal. Above all, Christ is his people's high priest.

By presenting Christ as his people's high priest the writer endeavours to make his readers understand the incomparable sufficiency of his work for them. He does not engage in unfounded speculation; he bases his argument on the Old Testament scriptures and on the well-known facts of what Jesus actually did, and appeals to what his readers had already proved in their own experience.

He himself, like his readers, appears to have been of Jewish origin. The idea of priesthood is therefore developed in the letter against the background of the Jewish priesthood. The Jewish priesthood had a long history of more than a thousand years, going back to Aaron, the brother of Moses. But if Jesus was to be presented as a priest against this background, a difficulty immediately arose. He belonged to the wrong tribe. All the Jewish priests had to belong to the tribe of Levi. But it was a matter of common knowledge, as the writer says, 'that our Lord was descended from Judah, and in connexion with that tribe [the tribe of Judah] Moses said nothing about priests' (Hebrews 7:14).

Happily, the writer knew an Old Testament text which made mention – and honourable mention – of another priesthood. Like several other New Testament writers, he applied to the exalted Jesus the oracle of Psalm 110:1, where God says to his anointed king, 'Sit at my right hand, till I make your enemies your footstool'. But he drew his readers' attention to another oracle in verse 4 of the same psalm, addressed presumably to the same person:

The LORD has sworn and will not change his mind, 'You are a priest for ever after the order of Melchizedek.'

Melchizedek was an ancient priest-king of Salem (Jerusalem) who, as we read in Genesis 14:18–20, bestowed a blessing on the patriarch Abraham and received from him the 'tithe' (one tenth) of all the property which Abraham had recently recovered from a plundering army of invaders. Plainly Melchizedek was a very great man. Centuries after the incident in which he figured, his city, Jerusalem, was taken by King David, who made it his capital. David thus became successor to the dynasty of which Melchizedek was the most illustrious representative. David belonged to the tribe of Judah, and so, therefore, did his descendant the Messiah, 'great David's greater Son'. There was therefore complete appropriateness in identifying Christ, of the tribe of Judah, with the one acclaimed by the divine oath as 'a priest for ever after the order of Melchizedek'. And part of the argument of the letter to the Hebrews is designed to show that the priest of Melchizedek's order is greater in every way than a priest of Aaron's line.

A sacrifice for sin

A priest represented his people before God, and in Jewish practice one of the principal ways in which he did so was the offering of sacrifices on their behalf. But Jesus is presented in this letter not just as a priest, but as a high priest. The high priest of Israel was specially associated with one particular sacrifice, which no one else could offer. This was the annual sin offering presented every autumn, on the Day of Atonement. To this day Jews observe this occasion as one of unsurpassed solemnity. They cannot now present a sin-offering, as sacrifices came to an end when the Jerusalem temple was destroyed in A.D. 70, but they observe the day as a fast-day, and call it (in Hebrew) *Yom Kippur* ('day of atonement').

What happened on the day of atonement? The ancient ritual is set out in the sixteenth chapter of Leviticus, which contemplates as the setting of the ritual the movable tent or tabernacle which served the Israelites as their sanctuary during their wilderness wanderings, in the days of Moses. In principle the same ritual was observed in the temple in Jerusalem, although minor modifications and elaborations had been introduced to suit changing circumstances. The temple in Jerusalem was still standing when the letter to the Hebrews was written, but the writer does not draw his information from what went on there year by year. Both he and his readers appear to have lived in the 'dispersion' – that is, in one of the areas of Jewish settlement outside Palestine. He draws his information from the Old Testament, especially from Leviticus 16. He and his readers were probably better acquainted with the Old Testament scriptures than they were with current Jerusalem practice.

The wilderness tabernacle, like the Jerusalem temple later, consisted of two compartments – an outer (and larger) compartment and an inner (and smaller) one. The outer compartment, the 'holy place', was entered by priests every day in fulfilment of their sacred duties. The inner compartment, the 'holy of holies', was entered by no one except the high priest, and he entered it only once a year, on the day of atonement.

On that day he entered it twice, on both occasions carrying in a basin the blood of sacrificed animals. The first animal – a bull – was sacrificed as a sin-offering for the high priest and his family; its blood was then taken into the holy of holies by the high priest and sprinkled in front of the mercy seat, the covering of the ark of the covenant. (So at least the directions in Leviticus run, but when the letter to the Hebrews was written the ark of the covenant, with the mercy seat, had been lost for over 600 years. There was then no place to sprinkle the atoning blood in the holy of holies except on the floor or the walls.) When the high priest had thus been ceremonially purified from sin, he went out and killed the second animal – a goat – as a sin offering for the people and re-entered the holy of holies with its blood, which he sprinkled in the presence of the invisible God in the same way. During both his visits to the holy of holies the small room was filled with the smoke of incense, so that the high priest's 'intrusion' into such a sacred place might be as unobtrusive as possible. When he came out the second time, the people whom he represented breathed a sigh of relief because he had emerged safely from such perilous nearness to the holiness of God; the atonement which had been made for their sins was valid for the next twelve months.

That did not exhaust the ceremonies of the day of atonement. When he had fulfilled his responsibilities in the holy of holies, the high priest had to lay his hands on a live goat, and confess over it the sins which the nation had committed during the past year. The goat was then driven out to the wilderness and encouraged to get lost, together with all the sins which had been symbolically unloaded on to it. (It is said that at a later date this encouragement took a more drastic form: the goat was driven over a precipice to make sure that it would not inadvertently come back with its load of sins into any place where people lived.) But of this goat, traditionally called the 'scapegoat', no mention is made in the letter to the Hebrews. Its author is concerned with the high priest's ministry in the holy of holies, which he regards as sadly ineffective.

The high priest himself was a sinner; that is why he had to present his own sin-offering before he was fit to present one on behalf of the people. He went through his duties in the holy of holies in fear and trembling. When he came out, he and the people were glad to think that all that was over for another year. But next year the same ceremony had to be gone through again, and the year after that, and so on indefinitely. Sooner or later one high priest would die, or give up his office for some other reason, and his successor had to repeat the annual ceremony. In this our author sees evidence that the work of atonement was never finished.

But in fact the work of atonement was never even begun. Atonement in the proper sense of the word belongs to the moral and spiritual realm. It involves the removal of sin, which is not an external pollution but something which stains the conscience within, and requires cleansing at the very heart of one's being. How could any form of animal sacrifice deal with this situation? 'It is impossible,' says our author, 'that the blood of bulls and goats should take away sins.' (Hebrews 10:4.)

This is one of those statements which need only to be made

for their truth to be self-evident. The English hymn-writer
Isaac Watts put it plainly when he wrote:

> Not all the blood of beasts
> On Jewish altars slain
> Could give the guilty conscience peace
> Or wash away our stain;
>
> But Christ, the heavenly Lamb,
> Takes all our sins away,
> A sacrifice of nobler name
> And richer blood than they.

Watts in these words draws a contrast between the work of
Christ and the cleansing rituals of Old Testament times, just
as the writer to the Hebrews had done before him. And in truth,
we have only to envisage the strange ceremonies enacted by
the Jewish high priest on the day of atonement to appreciate
how differently we think today about approaching God in
worship and receiving the forgiveness which he so readily grants
to those who confess their sins.

The finality of the gospel

For the special purpose which he has in view in composing
this letter, the writer to the Hebrews describes the work of Christ
in terms of priesthood and sacrifice. As he does so, however,
he emphasizes at each stage how different the work of Christ
is from that of the ancient priests of Israel, how infinitely his
achievement surpasses theirs.

A heavenly priesthood. Their priesthood was an earthly priesthood; his is a heavenly priesthood. 'If he were on earth, he would
not be a priest at all' (Hebrews 8:4), because he did not belong
to the priestly tribe. The earthly priesthood was filled by
members of the tribe of Levi. The priesthood of Christ, as our
author views the situation, began immediately after his death,
when he was raised to his present supremacy. This is the
moment envisaged in the oracle of Psalm 110:1, 'Sit at my right
hand, till I make your enemies your footstool.' It is equally

the moment envisaged in the companion oracle of Psalm 110:4, 'You are a priest for ever after the order of Melchizedek.'

Invested by oath. They were not invested with their priesthood by a divine oath, as Christ was invested with his. To him it is said: 'The Lord has *sworn*, and will not change his mind, "You are a priest for ever ..."' Even in this incidental distinction our author sees a token of the superiority of Christ's priesthood.

An undying priest. The priests of Israel, including the high priest, were mortal men. None of them could exercise his priesthood 'for ever', like the priest of Melchizedek's order; each of them, one after the other, had to die, and hand on his priesthood to another.

There is a moving story in Numbers 20:22–29 about the death of Aaron, the first high priest of Israel. Moses, by now a very old man, climbed Mount Hor with his brother Aaron (three years older than himself) and Aaron's son Eleazar. On the top of the mountain Moses stripped Aaron of his sacred vestments and put them on Eleazar. Aaron died there on the mountaintop, and Moses came down the hill with Eleazar and presented him to the people as their new high priest. So, generation by generation, the story in its essence was repeated; one priest died and another took his place.

How different it is with the Christians' high priest! He did indeed die, but now he is alive for evermore and holds his priesthood permanently; he needs no successor (Hebrews 7:25):

> Consequently he is able for all time to save those who draw near to God through him, since he always lives to make intercession for them.

A sinless priest. A more serious defect in the priests of Israel was that they were as much sinners as those whom they represented, and therefore had to bring sin-offerings for themselves as well as for their people. This was made outstandingly clear on the annual day of atonement. As we have seen, the high priest had to go into the holy of holies twice on that day. The first time he had to present the blood of his own sin-offering; only when he had done that could he perform the same ceremony for the sins of his people.

The Christians' high priest has no need to bring a sin-offering for himself. If he needed to bring such an offering, where could he find one? As it is, he is 'holy, blameless, unstained' (Hebrews 7:26). Yet this does not mean that he is unable to have a fellow-feeling with sinful men and women. He is 'one who in every respect has been tempted as we are, yet without sinning' (Hebrews 4:15). The strength of temptation is felt more by those who resist it than by those who yield to it. He who resisted it without ever yielding to it experienced its strength more than anyone else. He is thus well qualified to be the representative and intercessor for the human race in the presence of God; he knows what it is like to be human, for he was a real human being during his earthly life and he remains a real human being in his present exaltation.

If he were not a real human being he would be disqualified from acting as his people's high priest. He had to become completely like his people, sharing the same flesh-and-blood nature, in order not only to live with them but also to die for them. Having passed through death and triumphed over it, he is still the same Jesus as he was 'in the days of his flesh' – that is, during his life on earth – when 'with loud cries and tears' he poured out his soul in entreaty to God and had his prayer answered when he was brought back from death (Hebrews 5:7). If his people find the going hard, they may take courage from the realization that he too, Son of God though he was, 'learned obedience through what he suffered' (verse 8).

Then, as now, he stands before us (and before God) as a *sinless* human being; and this is of great importance. It is emphasized throughout this letter that sin, disobedience to God, is the one effective barrier to approaching him. One who is without sin, as Christ is, can approach him freely; and when Christ now approaches him freely he does so on his people's behalf as well as on his own.

A spiritual sanctuary. Another contrast to which our attention is drawn in this letter is that the priests of Israel ministered in an earthly and material sanctuary, while the Christians' high priest ministers in a heavenly sanctuary which belongs to the spiritual order. In this connexion our author thinks of the command of God in Exodus 25:40, where Moses receives detailed directions for the construction of the tabernacle and its furnishings and is told: 'see that you make them after the pattern for them, which is being shown you on the mountain' – that is, on Mount Sinai. Our author understands that Moses somehow saw an eternal and spiritual reality of which he (or others under his guidance) had to make a material copy. The priests of Israel ministered in the copy, but Christ ministers as high priest in the eternal and spiritual reality. The high priest of Israel passed through the material holy place on the day of atonement into the material holy of holies. Christ, on the other hand, has passed through a 'greater and more perfect tent (not made with hands, that is, not of this creation)' – in other words, he 'has passed through the heavens' – not to the earthly symbol of the throne of God (the ark of the covenant surmounted by the mercy seat) but 'into heaven itself, now to appear in the presence of God on our behalf' (Hebrews 9:11; 4:14; 9:24). The pictorial language which our author uses to depict Christ's entering into the heavenly sanctuary may make us think of some locality, some celestial dwelling, far more glorious than any earthly temple and situated on a higher plane, but visibly corresponding to the material sanctuary. Many years ago I listened to a lecture on the tabernacle of Moses' day, illustrated by a portable scale-model of the structure. As the lecturer explained its significance, he said, 'I have no doubt that, when we get to heaven, we shall see something exactly corresponding to this model.' I doubted it then, and I still do. We shall have a better idea of what is meant in this letter by the heavenly sanctuary, in which Christ ministers as his people's high priest, if we bear in mind simultaneously two things about it. First, it signifies the very presence of God; next, and at the same time, it signifies the fellowship of the people of God, even while they live on earth. How this can be so we shall see before long.

A once-for-all sacrifice. But first, no careful reader of the letter to the Hebrews can fail to mark the contrast between the endless repetition of the sacrifices prescribed by the law of Moses and the unrepeated and unrepeatable character of the sacrifice of Christ. The priests of Israel offered up sacrifices day by day or, in the case of the special sin-offering on the day of atonement, year by year. Christ, on the other hand, 'offered for all time a single sacrifice for sins' and 'entered once for all into the Holy Place' (Hebrews 10:12; 9:12). This, says our author, is why, 'when he had made purification for sins, he sat down at the right hand of the Majesty on high' (Hebrews 1:3), unlike those priests who remain standing in the discharge of their duties, because their sacrificial work is never done; it always has to be done again. What is there about the sacrifice of Christ that makes it unique?

The sacrifice of himself. First of all, his sacrifice was the sacrifice of himself. He was both priest and sacrifice in one. What inherent value could there be in the killing and offering up of dumb animals? They had no choice in the matter; they could have no conception of what was being done with them. They were entirely subject to the will of others. When Jesus, on the other hand, offered up his life to God as an offering for the sins of men and women, he did so intelligently and voluntarily. He deliberately dedicated his whole life to doing the will of God. Our author sees fulfilled in Jesus the language addressed to God in Psalm 40:6–8, which he quotes in this form (Hebrews 10:5–7):

> Sacrifice and offering thou hast not desired,
> but a body hast thou prepared for me;
> in burnt offerings and sin offerings thou hast taken no pleasure.
> Then I said, 'Lo, I have come to do thy will, O God',
> as it is written of me in the roll of the book.

In other words, it is not material offerings that God wants – whether the blood of slaughtered animals or anything else external to his worshippers – but the devotion of heart and will. And this is what he received in full measure from Jesus, from first to last. The death of Jesus was all of a piece with his life; it was an act of obedience which crowned all the obedience that preceded it. If animal sacrifices are irrelevant in God's sight, the offering up in death of a perfectly obedient life is, on the contrary, of infinite value. So, echoing the description of the obedient Servant of the Lord in Isaiah 53:12, our author says that Christ was 'offered once to bear the sins of many' (Hebrews 9:28).

So perfectly acceptable to God was the obedience of his Son, consummated in his death, that no other sacrifice for the sins of mankind is necessary. Hence our author emphasizes the contrast between the indefinitely repeated sacrifices offered in the earthly sanctuary and the fact that Christ 'appeared once for all at the end of the age [that is, at the time of fulfilment] to put away sin by the sacrifice of himself' (Hebrews 9:26).

Moreover, the sacrifice that is completely acceptable to God is completely effective in the lives of men and women. The trouble that needs to be put right lies in the moral and spiritual realm, and the action which puts it right must lie in that realm. It is a guilty conscience, a conscience stained with sin, that requires to be purified, and this kind of purification cannot be accomplished by animal sacrifices or any other cleansing ceremonies enacted with material agents. Such ceremonies can be at best but symbols of spiritual realities. But the sacrifice of Christ is the spiritual reality which purifies the consciences of those who come to him in faith, and enables them to enjoy unhindered access to God. To ensure this permanent access the exalted Christ is permanently engaged on his people's behalf.

The Christian's experience

This is the doctrine; what about the experience? Our author knew that his readers would recognize the truth of the doctrine he set forth because it corresponded to their actual experience. When they had put their faith in Christ they had actually experienced inward cleansing through his death and risen life; they had been purified in heart and conscience and now had no sense of inhibition when they approached God in worship and prayer.

The psalmist's words quoted above, which our author interprets of Christ's self-dedication to do the will of God, continue with the confession, 'thy law is within my heart' (Psalm 40:8). This is not included in his formal quotation, but its sense is woven into his argument. For Christ the law of God was not simply a code written in a book or on stone tablets; it was written in his heart in the sense that he spontaneously desired to do the things which the law of God commanded, whether or not those things were formally written down. But since they were in fact written down, their written record was, so to speak, a transcript of his character and conduct: 'as it is written of me in the roll of the book.' (Psalm 40:7.)

Now what was true of him has become true of those who have received inward purification through him: the law of God is now within their hearts too. And this clearly marks the fulfilment of God's promise to make a new covenant with his people in place of the old one under which the ancient ritual was instituted. The new covenant has been inaugurated by Christ, as the old one was introduced in the time of Moses. Our author recalls the occasion at the foot of Mount Sinai, recorded in Exodus 24:3–8, when Moses read the law to the people of Israel and they accepted its obligations. Moses (as we have seen) then sprinkled on them the blood of sacrificed animals and said, 'This is the blood of the covenant which God commanded you' (Hebrews 9:19–20). (See page 37.)

Half-way between Moses and Christ the divine promise of a new covenant to replace the old was given through the prophet Jeremiah, in an oracle (Jeremiah 31:31–34) which our author quotes in full (Hebrews 8:8–12). He particularly underlines two terms in this new covenant which bring out its superiority to the old one: first, God undertakes to write his law on his people's hearts, and secondly, he says in the last clause of the oracle, 'I will remember their sins no more.'

If God's law is written on his people's hearts, they will do his will voluntarily, and as for their previous sins, they are blotted out from his record. Under the old order, sins were remembered continually, and especially on the day of atonement; under the new order, past sins are forgotten.

What about sins committed subsequently? In so far as these are inadvertent, they are presumably dealt with by a heavenly high priest who can sympathize with his people's weaknesses. But in so far as they are deliberate, committed 'with a high hand' (as the Old Testament phrase puts it), no such provision is held out. When he speaks of such deliberate sinning, our author seems to have in mind something which amounts to apostasy, the repudiation of the faith formerly professed. Those who renounce the one and only effective sin-offering cannot expect to find atonement anywhere else.

The guardian of mankind

As for his present work, Christ is portrayed in this letter as exercising his high-priestly ministry in the heavenly sanctuary. The high priests of Israel did not linger in the earthly holy of holies; they completed their duties there and made haste to get away. But Christ, having accomplished his sacrificial death on earth, has entered the heavenly holy of holies and remained there, welcomed by God and enthroned (in the language of the psalm) at his right hand. The high priests of Israel carried the blood of sacrificed animals into the earthly holy of holies; otherwise they would not have dared to enter. But Christ has no need to carry sacrificial blood into the divine presence in the spiritual world; he has entered there by virtue of his perfect self-sacrifice and exercises his high-priestly ministry there on the basis of that sacrifice. That is why we said earlier that he does not simply pray for his people in heaven as he prayed for Peter on earth: his very presence in heaven, as the crucified and exalted one, constitutes the most eloquent and prevailing of prayers. Charles Wesley has expressed the idea in one of his great flights of poetic imagery:

> Five bleeding wounds he bears,
>   Received on Calvary,
> They pour effectual prayers,
>   They strongly speak for me:

'Forgive him, O forgive', they cry,
'Nor let that ransomed sinner die.'

We must not think of a suppliant Christ, tearfully pleading his people's cause before a reluctant God; we should think rather of an enthroned and exalted Christ, the representative of his people, one whose requests on their behalf are always gladly granted by the Father.

To know that their representative, 'the guardian of mankind', enjoys unique honour and favour in the presence of God is a powerful incentive to his people to avail themselves of the constant and free access which he has secured for them into the presence of God. 'Let us then,' says our author, 'with confidence draw near to the throne of grace, that we may receive mercy and find grace to help in time of need.' (Hebrews 4:16.) The realm into which Christ has passed is not inaccessible to his people. It is not simply one which they may look forward to entering at death; it is open to them here and now. If it is described as being high above all heavens, that is a figure of speech denoting its transcendence: it belongs to the spiritual order and is present everywhere and all the time to men and women of faith. The real and eternal sanctuary where Christ now ministers is identical with that house of God which is composed of all believers who hold fast their confidence and the glorying of their hope (Hebrews 3:6). Among them God dwells; of them he says, in the language of the covenant, 'I will be their God, and they shall be my people' (Hebrews 8:10).

The pioneer of faith

Here it is appropriate to think of another figure in which the present relationship between Christ and his people is set forth in this letter. They are called to embark upon a pilgrim's progress, making their way towards the city that is to come. This was the city towards which pilgrims in earlier days pressed forward: Abraham, for example, 'looked forward to the city which has foundations, whose maker and builder is God' (Hebrews 11:10). The pilgrimage calls for staying power and

faith. A good beginning is not sufficient. It is relatively easy
to start well in the enthusiasm of a new venture; the real test
of faith comes with the middle stages, which must be completed
if the goal is to be reached. But strong encouragement to
perseverance is provided by the example of Christ, the path-
finder or trail-blazer of this pilgrim way. This is why he is called
'the pioneer and perfecter' of faith. He not only blazed the trail
himself but completed the pilgrimage, enduring the cross as
he did so; and now he imparts to his followers the strength
and resolution to tread where he trod and to arrive where he
waits to welcome them, in the rest that is appointed for the
people of God.

Christ's reappearance

To revert to the analogy of the high priest: the worshippers
were glad each day of atonement when they saw their high priest
emerge safely from the sanctuary. The offering which he
presented on their behalf had been accepted for another year.
In the new age the people of Christ have no doubt about the
acceptance of their high priest and his self-offering. Nevertheless
they expect him to emerge from the heavenly sanctuary and
to appear once more on this earthly plane: 'he will appear a
second time,' says our author, 'not to deal with sin [which was
dealt with effectively and finally at his first coming] but to save
those who are eagerly waiting for him.' (Hebrews 9:28.) He who
'is able for all time to save those who draw near to God through
him' (Hebrew 7:25) will then bring his saving work to its consummation. With this hope our author encourages his readers
to keep looking to Jesus, to exercise endurance and receive the
full measure of all that God has promised them in Christ;
'for yet a little while, and the coming one shall come and not
delay' (Hebrews 10:37).

7

WORTHY IS THE LAMB

A book of pictures

The Revelation to John is, to many modern readers, the strangest book of the New Testament. That is mainly because it belongs to a class of literature which is not produced today, although it was common enough in the Near East during the three centuries between (say) 170 B.C. and A.D. 130. This class of literature is called 'apocalyptic', from the noun 'Apocalypse', which is an alternative term for Revelation (both terms mean 'unveiling'). In apocalyptic, great use is made of pictorial symbols – animals and so forth – which represent realities other than themselves. The people for whom such works were first composed understood these symbols, but for us it is not so easy. To discover their meaning calls for careful study. For example, in Revelation 12 we are introduced to a great red dragon which threatens a woman 'clothed with the sun' and tries to destroy her firstborn son and the rest of her children. (If her firstborn son is not explicitly said to be her firstborn, it is nevertheless implied in the context.) It is easy to identify the dragon with the devil, the age-old enemy of God and mankind, because this identification is made for us in the text. But who are the others? The woman is probably the true Israel, her firstborn son the Messiah, and the rest of her children Christians in general; but this would not be universally agreed. Again, the dragon energizes a ferocious wild beast with seven heads and ten horns, which wages war against the saints. There never was such a literal beast; what we have here is a symbolic figure for a pagan power, the Roman empire. The seven heads are seven emperors and the ten horns are ten other rulers, but when we try to identify these, certainty vanishes. The wild beast carries on its campaign of persecution against the saints beyond the stage reached when the Revelation was written, until their extermination seems inevitable. Then, when all hope seems gone, it is suddenly overcome and destroyed – and by a lamb, of all improbable figures! But we know who the lamb is: the lamb is a symbol of Jesus, submitting to suffering and death, and in so doing, winning the crowning victory of all time.

The Revelation, then, bears its own distinctive witness to the work of Christ, in its past, present and future aspects.

Creation and redemption

When Christ is designated as 'the Amen, ... the beginning of God's creation' (Revelation 3:14), he is depicted in the role of eternal Wisdom, possessed by God as 'the beginning of his way' (Proverbs 8:22) before heaven or earth were formed (see page 98). The title 'the Amen' may represent the word rendered 'master workman' in Proverbs 8:30, where Wisdom claims to have assisted the Creator in this capacity.

But much more emphasis is laid in Revelation on Christ's work of redemption than on his work of creation. In an opening doxology John ascribes everlasting glory and dominion 'to him who loves us and has freed us from our sins by his blood and made us a kingdom of priests to his God and Father' (Revelation 1:5–6). This language is elaborated in John's description of God's heavenly throne-room in the fourth and fifth chapters of the book. Caught up there in vision, he sees the enthroned Creator and hears the unceasing song of celestial beings (Revelation 4:11):

> Worthy art thou, our Lord and God,
> to receive glory and honour and power,
> for thou didst create all things,
> and by thy will they existed and were created.

This is an ancient song: it has been sung ever since first 'the morning stars sang together, and all the sons of God shouted for joy' (Job 38:7).

But as John takes everything in, he sees a sealed scroll in the right hand of God, and knows without being told that the hidden writing on this scroll sets out God's purpose of judgement and mercy for the world. He knows, too, that this purpose cannot be put into effect unless someone comes forward with the necessary authority to receive the scroll from God, break its seals, unroll it and read its contents. A loud voice rings forth (Revelation 5:2), 'Who is worthy to open the scroll and break its seals?' – but no one appears to claim that right. John bursts into tears, as though for fear that the divine purpose will never be fulfilled. Then one of the heavenly bystanders bids him dry his tears, because 'the Lion of the tribe of Judah' has won the victory which entitles him to take the scroll and read it. The lion was the emblem of the tribe of Judah; 'the Lion of the tribe of Judah' could only be the Messiah of David's royal line, since Judah was David's tribe. Overjoyed at the news, John looks around to see the conquering hero come. Sure enough, a symbolic animal makes its solemn entrance, but John sees no lion – he sees a *lamb*, a lamb fresh from the place of slaughter, with the fatal wound still open and unhealed. But the lamb has plainly come back to life, for it goes up to the throne and is given the scroll. And now all heaven bursts into praise once again; this time, however, it is not the ancient song of creation that John hears, but the 'new song' of redemption (Revelation 5:9–10):·

> Worthy art thou to take the scroll and to open its seals,
>   for thou wast slain and by thy blood didst ransom for God
>   some from every tribe and tongue and people and nation,
>   and hast made them a kingdom and priests to our God,
>   and they shall reign on earth.

The meaning of this 'new song' is plain: Christ has won the decisive victory of the ages, and he has won it through patient submission to violent death. There was a practical lesson here for those Christians who, when John wrote, were suffering persecution and martyrdom at the hands of the Roman empire. The way of victory which their Master found would be their way of victory too; they were to follow the Lamb wherever he led. As they did so, it was recorded of them that they conquered their enemies 'by the blood of the Lamb and by the word of their testimony, for they loved not their lives even unto death' (Revelation 12:11). That is to say, they put loyalty to Christ before their love of life, and died in consequence. But did they conquer? They did: in the end it was the Roman empire that capitulated to Christ, and not the Christians to the empire.

For here is another practical lesson to be learned from John's vision: the sacrifice of Christ guarantees the triumph of God's purpose in the world. Of the suffering Servant of the Lord it was said in Old Testament times that 'the will of the LORD shall prosper in his hand' (Isaiah 53:10). It is to him, because of his death on the cross, that world dominion belongs – not to the clenched fist but to the pierced hand. Jesus, not Caesar (any Caesar, then or since), is lord of history. 'Worthy is the Lamb who was slain, to receive power and wealth and wisdom and might and honour and glory and blessing!' (Revelation 5:12). 'The future is ours, brothers,' those first-century Christians *might* have said to one another; what they *did* say was 'Our Lamb has conquered; let us follow him.' Their triumph through suffering was part of the work of Christ; he triumphed in them.

Two points of view

One commentator on Revelation has reminded us of a scene in John Bunyan's *Pilgrim's Progress*, where Christian visits the Interpreter's House and is shown a number of object-lessons.

> Then I saw in my dream that the Interpreter took Christian by the hand, and led him into a place where was a fire burning against a wall, and one standing by it, always casting much water upon it, to quench it; yet did the fire burn higher and hotter.

Christian might well be amazed at this, and spectators might equally have been amazed at the capacity for survival shown by the followers of Christ in spite of all the efforts of Nero and others to extinguish them. When Christian asked, 'What means this?' –

> The Interpreter . . . had him about to the backside of the wall, where he saw a man with a vessel of oil in his hand, of the which he did also continually cast, but secretly, into the fire.

When Christian asked again, 'What means this?' he was told that the man who kept the fire alive with his constant supply of oil was Christ, maintaining 'with the oil of his grace' the saving work so well begun.

Similarly in the visions of Revelation we see the apparently hopeless plight of believers on earth, threatened with extermination by a power far greater than their own; but we also see the situation from the viewpoint of heaven, and understand how they are sustained and enabled to overcome by a still greater power – the power of their Leader who has already won the decisive victory over his enemies and theirs. John presses ancient symbolism into service to describe the determined efforts of the powers of evil to hinder and frustrate God's purpose in the world. But their malignant assaults are resisted and defeated by 'the endurance and faith of the saints', until at last the end of the war is proclaimed: 'The kingdom of the world has become the kingdom of our Lord and of his Christ, and he shall reign for ever and ever.' (Revelation 11:15.) No more fitting response could be made to this proclamation than the 'Hallelujah Chorus': 'Alleluia! for the Lord God omnipotent reigneth.' (Revelation 19:6; Authorized Version.)

The final triumph

In the past, then, Christ had suffered and overcome personally; in the present he was suffering and overcoming in his faithful followers. And in the future he would be manifested as the overcomer-in-chief, and they would be associated with him as

overcomers too. This ultimate overcoming is pictured by John
in an extraordinary scene. An Old Testament prophet had
described a divine warrior returning from the slaughter of his
enemies, whose life-blood stains his clothes: 'Who is this that
comes from Edom, in crimsoned garments from Bozrah?'
(Isaiah 63:1–6). John takes up the description, and presents
Christ as a victorious warrior, 'clad in a robe dipped in blood,
and the name by which he is called is The Word of God'
(Revelation 19:13). But, since John has already told us the secret
of this warrior's victory, we know that the blood which stains
his garments is his own and that of his followers, who shared
his victory in their turn 'by the blood of the Lamb and by the
word of their testimony'. The persecution of his followers,
following on his own execution, was designed to wipe out his
name and his cause from the face of the earth. Instead, his
death, followed by their martyrdom, ensured the survival of
his name and the victory of his cause. John's transformation
of the picture of the bloodstained warrior is not so revolutionary
as his Master's transformation of double defeat (as it seemed
to be) into victory.

To suppose that he who overcame once for all by his unresist-
ing submission to death will achieve his final victory by inflicting
suffering and death on others is to charge him not only with
a change of method but with a change of character. Yet a note
of sternness is present in John's depicting of the future work
of Christ. The carol which reminds us that

> Heaven and earth shall flee away
> When he comes to reign

draws these words from John's picture of the last judgement
before the great white throne on which is seated one from whose
presence 'earth and sky fled away' (Revelation 20:11). As the
gospel of John presents the Son of God as his Father's agent
in the passing of judgement, so the Revelation describes how,
on the great day of retribution, men call to the mountains and
rocks to fall on them and hide them 'from the face of him who

is seated on the throne, and from the wrath of the Lamb' (Revelation 6:16).

This phrase, 'the wrath of the Lamb', is such a surprising one that it deserves to be considered with care. If ever there was a contradiction in terms, surely this is it. One theologian of our own day, Professor A. T. Hanson, has written a whole book on divine judgement bearing the title *The Wrath of the Lamb*. In the Revelation, as in so many other books of the Bible, salvation and judgement go closely together. To repudiate Christ's salvation is to embrace his judgement. One of his last utterances in the Revelation is, 'Behold, I am coming soon, bringing my recompense, to repay every one for what he has done.' To this John adds his word of invitation: 'Let him who is thirsty come, let him who desires take the water of life without price.' (Revelation 22:12, 17.) This is not only an echo of the prophet's call, 'Ho, every one who thirsts, come to the waters...' (Isaiah 55:1); it repeats Jesus' own invitation of John 7:37 –

> He that is athirst, let him come to me;
> and let him drink who believes in me!

While Christ's 'strange work' of judgement is by no means soft-pedalled, his saving work, the work properly congenial to him, occupies the forefront in Revelation as it does elsewhere in the New Testament.

8

BEFORE THE INCARNATION

Christ in creation

In chapter 6 we saw that the writer of the letter to the Hebrews presents Christ as the eternal Son through whom God brought the world of space and time into being, and by whose enabling word the universe is sustained moment by moment.

It must come as a surprise to people reading the New Testament for the first time to discover how many of its writers use language like this. In the most matter-of-fact way they tell us that Jesus Christ, who lived and died in the first century A.D., had a hand in the creation of the world. They do not think it necessary to prove this; they simply state it. But what would make them conceive such an idea? It is not the sort of thing that would naturally be thought or said about any other figure in history.

The fact that several of them use this kind of language, in apparent independence of one another, suggests that it goes back to the earliest days of Christianity. That people could believe this about Jesus Christ, within perhaps ten or twenty years of his death, at least bears witness to the impact which he made on the minds of his followers.

John the evangelist, writing his gospel (as is commonly supposed) towards the end of the first century, starts off by declaring Jesus Christ, true man of woman born, to be the incarnation of the 'Word' or self-revelation of God which existed 'in the beginning' – for as long as God himself existed. If you understand this, he says to his readers in effect, you will understand many features in the ministry of Jesus that would otherwise be difficult to explain.

It is widely recognized that the English term 'Word' is hardly adequate to convey the fullness of John's meaning, but there is no single English term that would be any more adequate. The 'Word' in this sense is more than God's utterance or even self-expression; it is his agent, and because it is viewed as his *personal* agent it is more properly called 'he' than 'it'. The 'Word', for example, was God's agent 'in the beginning' when he created heaven and earth: 'all things were made through him, and without him was not anything made that was made.' (John 1:3.)

Where could this idea have come from? One probable source is the Old Testament. The first chapter of Genesis affirms repeatedly that 'God *said*' – and what he said was immediately translated into fact. 'God said, "Let there be light"; and there was light. ... God said, "Let us make man".... So God created man in his own image...; male and female he created them.' (Genesis 1:3, 26, 27.) If things were created because of what God *said*, then they were created by his *word*. So it is put in one of the psalms (Psalm 33:6, 9):

> By the word of the Lord the heavens were made,
>   and all their host by the breath of his mouth....
> For he spoke, and it came to be;
>   he commanded, and it stood forth.

Once Jesus is acknowledged as the Word of God, it might be said, then whatever is ascribed to the activity of the Word can truly be ascribed to him. As the Word of God, he existed before becoming incarnate in manhood.

If John wrote towards the end of the first Christian century, this conception of Jesus as the incarnation of the creative Word could be thought to be the fruit of his mature thinking. But the same essential conception appears much earlier than the end of the century. It may have been thirty years before the gospel of John was written that the writer to the Hebrews said that the Son, by whom God has spoken his final word to mankind, is the one 'whom he appointed heir of all things, through whom also he created the world. He reflects the glory of God and bears the very stamp of his nature, upholding the universe by his word of power' (Hebrews 1:2–3). We looked earlier (page 28) at the significance of Jesus' words in John 5:17, 'My Father is working still, and so I am working too.' The Father, that is to say, did not cease from working when he had created the universe; he continued to work by sustaining what he had created. And if the Son was the Father's agent in the former work, he has remained the Father's agent in the latter work. So, while the writer to the Hebrews and John the evangelist probably knew nothing of each other's writing, they are in remarkable agreement on this primeval phase of the work of Christ.

Some years before the letter to the Hebrews comes Paul's letter to the Colossians, which makes a full and explicit statement on this subject. Speaking of Christ at an early stage in this letter, Paul says (Colossians 1:15–18):

> He is the image of the invisible God, the first-born of all creation; for in him all things were created, in heaven and on earth, visible and invisible, whether thrones or dominions or principalities or powers – all things were created through him and for him. He is before all things, and in him all things hold together...; he is the beginning....

The statement that Christ is 'the image of the invisible God' is no mere theorizing on Paul's part: when the risen and glorified Christ appeared to him on the Damascus road, that was how he appeared. Paul recognized in him on that occasion the visible form of the God whom none can see. He had seen, as he puts it elsewhere, 'the light of the gospel of the glory of Christ, who is the image of God' (2 Corinthians 4:4).

When he specifies, among the 'all things' which were created through Christ and for him, 'thrones, dominions, principalities and powers', he has in mind those forces in the spiritual realm to which reference has been made in chapter 5 – those forces from whose tyranny believers in Christ are delivered through his victory. Here he says that those forces which in due course were defeated by Christ on the cross were in the first instance created through him. Either way, he is far superior to them, and those who are united to him by faith need pay them no allegiance.

But what of the comprehensive statement that in Christ 'all things were created'? The whole passage in which these words occur has been identified by some scholars as a primitive Christian hymn, which is being quoted in the letter because of its suitability to the context. If that is so, then it could be some years earlier than the letter, which should perhaps be dated about A.D. 60. In any case, five years previously Paul had embodied a brief confession of faith in 1 Corinthians 8:6 –

> for us there is one God, the Father, from whom are all things and for whom we exist; and one Lord, Jesus Christ, through whom are all things and through whom we exist.

This confession about Jesus Christ, 'through whom are all things and through whom we exist,' is more fully unpacked in the statement in Colossians.

But whether in Colossians Paul is quoting an already existent hymn, or composing in his own choice of words, his thought and language owe something to the portrayal of divine wisdom in the Old Testament. Hebrew psalmists and wise men acknowledged that the wisdom of God was displayed in his works of creation:

> O LORD, how manifold are thy works!
> In wisdom hast thou made them all; (Psalm 104:24)

> The LORD by wisdom founded the earth;
> by understanding he established the heavens. (Proverbs 3:19)

But at times divine wisdom is personified, even speaking in the first person singular as 'I'. Since 'wisdom' in Hebrew (and in Greek and Latin) is a noun in the feminine gender, personified Wisdom in the Old Testament is a female, the eldest daughter of the Almighty. This is the role in which Wisdom is made to speak in a frequently quoted passage (Proverbs 8:22–31), where she claims to have enjoyed the company of God 'before the beginning of the earth' and to have been present with him as a 'master workman' when he created the world. The passage begins:

> The Lord possessed me as the beginning of his way,
> before his works of old.

Now, quite apart from this creative role of divine wisdom, Christ is called 'the wisdom of God' in the New Testament: 'Christ Jesus, whom God made our wisdom' (1 Corinthians 1:30). This may be based on Christ's own authority, for those were times when he spoke recognizably as the wisdom of God: some of his utterances have been classified as 'wisdom sayings'. But when Christ is called the wisdom of God, this is no mere personification such as we find in the Old Testament. Personification is a figure of speech, but when Christ is called the wisdom of God, what is meant is that this real person is the embodiment of divine wisdom. Divine wisdom was manifested in all his works and words during his public ministry, and pre-eminently in his crucifixion (preposterous as such a claim was bound to appear by the standards of ordinary human wisdom).

Once Christ was identified as the *personal* wisdom of God, the activities of *personified* wisdom in the Old Testament were naturally ascribed to him. The opening words of Proverbs 8:22 seem to mean, 'The Lord possessed me (not *in* or *at*, but) *as* the beginning of his way'; and this claim probably underlies the statement of Colossians 1:18, 'he is the beginning.' The same claim, we have seen already (page 88), underlies Revelation 3:14, where the risen Christ, addressing the church of Laodicea, introduces himself as 'the Amen, the faithful and true witness, *the beginning of God's creation*'.

Christ, then, is 'the beginning'. But there is another creation passage in the Old Testament where the word 'beginning' appears. That is the first chapter of Genesis, which opens with the statement that 'in the beginning God created the heavens and the earth'. Now, it might be argued, if Christ is 'the beginning', then it was in him that the heavens and the earth were created. This is precisely what is affirmed in Colossians 1:16: 'in him all things were created.'

But if this was how those early Christians reasoned, it was no empty speculation. The eternal wisdom which became man in Jesus of Nazareth was the wisdom by which God had brought the world into being; the God who had spoken his creative and self-revealing word in the beginning was the God who had now revealed himself in Jesus Christ to inaugurate a new creation through him. When it is stated that Christ was the agent in the old creation, the purpose is to make that serve as a back-cloth for his work in the new creation. For, to quote Paul, 'it is the God who said, "Let light shine out of darkness," who has shone in our hearts to give the light of the knowledge of the glory of God in the face of Christ.' (2 Corinthians 4:6.)

Christ with Israel in the wilderness

Another example of this 'pre-incarnate' work of Christ finds mention here and there in the New Testament. As early Christians read the Old Testament, they found an impressive series of parallels between their own experiences and those of the people of Israel during their wilderness wanderings on the way from Egypt to Canaan. The Israelites' experiences had been on the earthly level, whereas those of the early Christians were on the spiritual level; but the former served as a kind of allegory in advance for the latter. The Israelites' slave-labour under Pharaoh corresponded to the Christians' earlier bondage to sin; the Israelites' deliverance by the blood of the passover lamb corresponded to the Christians' deliverance when Christ, their passover, was sacrificed for them; the Israelites' passing through the 'sea of reeds' corresponded to Christian baptism; the manna on which they fed and the water which they drank from the rock corresponded to the bread and the cup in the Lord's Supper. The promised land to which the Israelites journeyed symbolized the heavenly 'rest that remains for the people of God' (see page 86), but just as many Israelites who set out from Egypt were unable to enter the promised land because of unbelief and disobedience to God, some professing Christians might forfeit *their* goal for the same reason.

So far, so good; but this series of correspondences, used as a basis for solemn warnings by more than one New Testament writer, does not in itself involve the work of Christ. One of those writers, however, seems to make Jesus an active participant in the events of the wilderness wanderings. Jude, in his short letter, reminds his readers that '*Jesus*, who saved a people out of the land of Egypt, afterwards destroyed those who did not believe' (Jude 5). This seemed such an extraordinary statement to many early editors and copyists of the New Testament that they changed 'Jesus' to 'the Lord' or 'God' or simply 'he'; many modern translations adopt one or another of these variant readings. But 'Jesus' remains in enough manuscripts and other authorities to make it certain that this is what Jude originally wrote: if Jude had written one of the other readings, no scribe would have changed it to 'Jesus'.

But if Jude wrote 'Jesus', what did he mean? 'Jesus' is the Greek word for Joshua, and in the two places where Joshua is mentioned by name in the New Testament the Authorized Version calls him 'Jesus' (Acts 7:45; Hebrews 4:8). But Joshua's responsibility began at the end of the wilderness wanderings; he had no share in bringing the Israelites out of Egypt. It cannot be to him that Jude refers. Jude refers to the death, by plague and otherwise, of nearly the whole adult generation that came out of Egypt – 'this evil generation', as it is called in Deuteronomy 1:35 – and represents it as a work of judgement performed by Jesus long centuries before his incarnation.

A more beneficent contribution by Jesus to the Israelites in their wanderings is mentioned by Paul. Referring to the water from the rock which was provided for them, he says that they 'drank from the spiritual Rock which accompanied them, and the Rock was Christ' (1 Corinthians 10:4). Paul's language is sometimes explained in terms of a rabbinical fancy, which arose from the fact that there are two accounts in the Old Testament of the water from the rock – one at the beginning of the wilderness wanderings (Exodus 17:1–7) and one towards the end, nearly forty years later (Numbers 20:2–13). This rabbinical fancy reckoned that it was the same rock on both occasions – a mobile rock which accompanied the people all the way through the wilderness. But this is not what Paul has in mind when he speaks of 'the spiritual Rock which accompanied them'. To him the literal rock was the symbol of a spiritual reality, the spiritual reality being the presence of Christ: 'the Rock,' he says, 'was Christ.' It was Christ, in other words, who accompanied his people then in the wilderness, just as he continues to accompany his people today. This is what Christians mean when they sing:

> Guide me, O thou great Redeemer,
> Pilgrim through this barren land.

Christians today have good reason to claim the presence of Christ in this way; they remember his parting words to his followers: 'lo, I am with you always, to the close of the age.' (Matthew 28:20.) But what made Paul and Jude speak of Christ as being present with the Israelites in the wilderness? If they had followed the strict letter of the Old Testament record they might have spoken of the angel of the Lord as accompanying them – the angel of whom God said, 'My name is in him,' (Exodus 23:20–21) – or the presence of the Lord – 'My presence will go with you,' said God (Exodus 33:14) – or, combining the two expressions, 'the angel of his presence' (Isaiah 63:9). It seems plain, however, that Paul and Jude understood the 'presence' of God, the messenger in whom his 'name' was, to be identical with the Son of God who in the fullness of time became incarnate as Jesus of Nazareth.

These very occasional hints in the New Testament were developed in a big way by some Christian writers in the second century, and their example has been followed in succeeding centuries, not excluding our own. Some writers have allowed their imagination to run riot on this subject: others have preserved a more sober measure of discipline. The author of *The Wrath of the Lamb*, a book which has been mentioned earlier (page 93) has written another book entitled *Jesus Christ in the Old Testament*, in which he refers to the 'real presence' of Christ as a principle of interpretation in Old Testament history, a principle for which he finds authority in the New Testament. So far as New Testament authority is concerned, the principle is perhaps not so pervasive as he suggests. Our concern, however, is with what the *Bible* teaches about the work of Christ, and we have seen some pointers in the New Testament to a 'pre-incarnate' work of Christ in the Old Testament, a work of creation, salvation and judgement.

But like his agency in creation, his ministry to his people in the wilderness is also treated as the back-cloth to the ministry which he discharges, as the crucified and enthroned Lord, on his people's behalf today.

9

THE WITNESS OF PROPHECY

When the New Testament writers speak of the work of Christ in the Old Testament, it is not so much with reference to his occasional 'pre-incarnate' participation in the history of Israel as to the fact that prophets and psalmists spoke in advance of his 'incarnate' work.

The church's earliest Bible

Let us remember that the Old Testament was the church's Bible in the earliest period of its existence. When Jesus himself, and the apostles after him, looked for Bible texts on which to base the gospel which they preached, they found them in abundance – in the Old Testament. Right on into the second century, until the New Testament documents were gathered together and began to circulate as a collection supplementing the Old Testament, this continued to be the pattern. In evangelization, in defence of the faith, and in the encouragement of Christians, the Old Testament provided all the basic scriptural authority that was found to be necessary. And that was not all. The form in which the Old Testament was used was a Greek translation made from the original Hebrew a century or two before the birth of Christ. This translation – commonly called the Septuagint – was made in the first instance for the use of Greek-speaking Jews living outside Palestine, around the shores of the Eastern Mediterranean; but it was read by non-Jews also. And one of the most extraordinary features of the church's expansion in the second century A.D. is the number of educated pagans who were converted, not to Judaism but to Christianity, by reading the Old Testament.

Jews and Christians alike at that time read the same Old Testament, but read it, so to speak, through different spectacles and so could not agree about its meaning. Christians read it through Christian spectacles – that is to say, Jesus and the apostles had taught them how to read it so as to see the gospel there.

Thus, when Paul summarizes in 1 Corinthians 15:3–8 the gospel which he and the other apostles preached, he insists that the two great saving events on which it rested – Christ's death and resurrection – took place 'in accordance with the scriptures', by which the Old Testament scriptures are meant. The same Paul is portrayed in Acts as telling King Agrippa that throughout his preaching ministry he said 'nothing but what the prophets and Moses said would come to pass: that the Christ must suffer, and that, by being the first to rise from the dead, he would proclaim light both to the [Jewish] people and to the Gentiles.' (Acts 26:22–23.) Nor is Paul the only New Testament preacher to use such language. In 1 Peter 1:11 it is affirmed that the principal theme of the Old Testament prophets was 'the sufferings of Christ and the subsequent glory', and that the power which enabled them to foresee the sufferings and the glory was 'the Spirit of Christ within them'.

If we turn to the gospels, we discover that the evangelists, especially Matthew, find not only the death and resurrection of Christ but earlier phases of his career foretold in the Old Testament. Matthew sees incidents in his birth and infancy as recapitulating incidents described in advance by the prophets, and when he comes to record the public work of Christ he illustrates various aspects of it in greater detail from the book of Isaiah in particular. Jesus' Galilean ministry is said to fulfil the passage in Isaiah 9:1–2 about 'Galilee of the Gentiles', where 'the people who sat in darkness have seen a great light' (Matthew 4:15–16). The unobtrusiveness of Jesus' ministry is said to fulfil the description of the Servant of the Lord in Isaiah 42:1–4 as one who 'will not wrangle or cry aloud', who 'will not break a bruised reed or quench a smouldering wick' (Matthew 12:18–21). His healing of the sick and demon-possessed is said to fulfil a further description of the Servant in Isaiah 53:4 as the one who 'took our infirmities and bore our diseases' (Matthew 8:17). His teaching by means of parables is said to fulfil the psalmist's announcement in Psalm 78:2, 'I will open my mouth in parables' (Matthew 13:35). And so we might go on. Matthew does more of this sort of thing than the other evangelists do, but they all do it in measure. Like Paul and Peter and other New Testament writers they are sure that the prophets spoke in advance of the earthly work of Christ.

Jesus and the Son of Man

What was the origin of this conviction which they all shared? The gospels themselves offer us an answer to this question. They all assure us that Jesus himself claimed that his ministry, especially his death, was foretold in the Old Testament writings. According to Luke, when Jesus made his first public appearance in Nazareth, he announced the programme of his ministry in the words of Isaiah 61:1–2 (quoted above on page 21). According to the same evangelist, when he entered into conversation with the two disciples on the Emmaus road on his resurrection day, he explained to them 'in all the scriptures' how necessary it was that the Messiah should suffer before entering into his glory (Luke 24:25–27). According to Mark's gospel, the earliest of the four, he emphasized that 'it is *written* of the Son of man, that he should suffer many things and be treated with contempt' (Mark 9:12), and, as we have already seen (page 38), he submitted to his captors in the garden of Gethsemane with the words: 'Let the scriptures be fulfilled.' (Mark 14:49.)

Jesus' insistence that his saving work, and especially his suffering and death, fulfilled what had been written beforehand is firmly embedded in the gospel record – too firmly for us to suppose that it was later ascribed to him by others. Others may have dotted the i's and crossed the t's of his own teaching in this matter, but it was he who set the example which so many were to follow, when he emphasized that 'the Son of Man must suffer' – the 'must' being the 'must' of the divine purpose, communicated to the prophets and preserved in their writings.

What scriptures, then, were fulfilled by his submission to suffering and death?

Son of Man and Servant of the Lord

The Old Testament writers do not say in so many words that 'the Son of man must suffer'. If we have been right in thinking (page 18) that behind Jesus' references to the Son of Man lies Daniel's vision of 'one like a son of man' who receives world dominion from God (Daniel 7:13), it must be agreed that Daniel does not describe this figure as suffering. True, Daniel's 'one like a son of man' is the head or representative of 'the saints of the Most High' – and *they* certainly suffer. Daniel in his vision saw a 'little horn' on the head of a wild beast, representing a pagan tyrant, which 'made war with the saints, and prevailed over them' (Daniel 7:21), and it could easily be argued that if the saints had to endure this assault, their representative leader had to endure it too.

But the Son of Man not only suffers; he is rejected or treated with contempt. And this gives us the clue to the thought in Jesus' mind. For there is one figure in Old Testament prophecy who is explicitly said to be rejected and treated with contempt. That is the Servant of the Lord, of whom it is said, 'He was despised and rejected by men; ... he was despised, and we esteemed him not' (Isaiah 53:3). If Jesus united in his thinking the Son of Man and the Servant of the Lord, then much that he says about the Son of Man becomes readily understood, especially his assertion that '*it is written* of the Son of Man that he must suffer many things and be treated with contempt'.

Why should Jesus accept the experience of the humiliated and outcast Servant as the 'work' which he was to undertake?

Certainly, he had been acclaimed by the heavenly voice at his baptism in terms which showed him that his messianic destiny was to be achieved along the path marked out for the Servant. But the heavenly voice echoed the opening words of Isaiah 42; was there any reason to conclude that these words meant that he was to undergo the suffering described in Isaiah 53? God speaks of more servants than one in the book of Isaiah; is there any indication that the Servant of Isaiah 53 is identical with the Servant of Isaiah 42?

There is good reason to identify them. In Isaiah 42:1 God introduces the Servant with the words 'Behold my servant'. And the oracle which begins in Isaiah 52:13 and goes on to the end of chapter 53 opens with the same words of introduction: again God says, 'Behold my servant'. (Today we commonly refer to Isaiah 42:1–4 as the first Servant Song and Isaiah 52:13–53:12 as the fourth Servant Song.) By the laws of interpretation which were accepted in Israel in those days, those identical words of introduction made it clear that the same Servant was intended in both places. Practically every Old Testament scholar today would agree that the same Servant is intended; and Jesus knew not only that the same Servant was intended, but that he himself was to fulfil what was written about that Servant.

It was not simply that he recognized the programme of his ministry written down in advance in a book for him to follow. To do what he actually did, to endure what he actually endured, was the spontaneous desire of his heart. Nothing would have been more foreign or uncongenial to his nature than to embrace some other way – the way of political power, armed rebellion, or military conquest, for example. If we find it impossible to envisage Jesus in any of these roles, we are guided by a sound instinct. The way which he knew to be his Father's will for him was the way of his own choice.

'The chastisement that made us whole'

It was not simply in the *fact* of suffering that Jesus fulfilled

what was written about the Servant of the Lord. He fulfilled
it also in the *purpose* of his suffering.

Why does the Servant of the Lord suffer in Isaiah 53? And
what is the effect of his suffering? At one time there were people
who thought the Servant was suffering for his own sins; that
God was displeased with him and was punishing him. (Job's
friends, incidentally, had the same wrong idea about Job's
suffering.) But those wrong ideas about the Servant's suffering
gave way in due course to the realization of the truth. It was
not for his own sins, but for the sins of others, that he suffered.
And those who realized that this was so expressed their new
and better understanding in these words (Isaiah 53:4–6):

> Surely he has borne our griefs
>   and carried our sorrows;
> yet we esteemed him stricken,
>   smitten by God, and afflicted.
> But he was wounded for our transgressions,
>   he was bruised for our iniquities;
> upon him was the chastisement that made us whole,
>   and with his stripes we are healed.
> All we like sheep have gone astray;
>   we have turned every one to his own way;
> and the LORD has laid on him
>   the iniquity of us all.

If it is the Lord who 'has laid on him the iniquity of us all',
the context makes it plain that this was no unwelcome burden,
resented by the one who had to bear it. On the contrary, the
Servant's will in this matter (as in all others) was completely
at one with the will of God. And the words just quoted indicate
also that the Servant did not simply suffer because others had
sinned; he suffered for their benefit. 'Upon him,' they confess,
'was the chastisement that made us whole.' And how did his
chastisement heal them? Because the Servant accepted, or
absorbed, in his own person the judgement which their sins
had earned, as well as the sins themselves. 'When he makes
himself an offering for sin,' says God through the prophet,
'...my righteous servant will justify many, and he will bear

their iniquities' (Isaiah 53:10–11). And the closing words of the prophecy foretell the Servant's vindication and triumph (Isaiah 53:12) –

> because he poured out his soul to death,
>   and was numbered with the transgressors;
> yet he bore the sin of many,   —
>   and made intercession for the transgressors.

Late in the 1880s a boy in his teens who was learning shorthand made a virtue, as he thought, of the necessity of attending a church service by taking down the sermon in shorthand. To begin with, he was much more interested in this exercise than in what the preacher was saying. But the preacher had chosen part of Isaiah 53 as his text, and as he went on, the boy found himself captivated by the vision of Christ's incomparable grace that was unfolded. 'As the preacher reached his end, the hearer resolved to make his beginning, as a disciple of Him who is still despised and rejected of men.' It is good to know that, even so, 'his hand kept pace with the preacher's words to the very end'! But when that boy grew up, he became a distinguished Old Testament scholar, Dr Henry Wheeler Robinson, and one of his books is entitled *The Cross in the Old Testament*. (It is in one of the divisions of that book, called 'The Cross of the Servant', that he gives us this piece of autobiography.)

We may say that in these chapters of the book of Isaiah we are given a portrait of God's perfect servant, a portrait which remained an ideal until, when the time was fully come, it was transformed into reality by the life and death of Jesus Christ.

There is no doubt that many, perhaps most, of the New Testament writers saw in Jesus the fulfilment of that prophecy about the Servant of the Lord; they not only allude to it but several of them actually quote from it. The fact that this interpretation is common to so many of them suggests that it goes back beyond them all to Jesus himself, and this is confirmed by the record of the gospels. We have said already that his insistence that the Son of Man must suffer and be rejected is best understood if in his mind the Son of Man was fused with the Servant of the Lord. On the occasion when a paralysed man was let down by his friends through a hole in the roof of the house where Jesus was, Jesus not only cured him but assured him that his sins were forgiven. This was, he said, so that people might know that 'the Son of Man has authority on earth to forgive sins' (Mark 2:10). Daniel's 'one like a son of man' receives authority to pronounce *judgement*, but how has he authority to pronounce *forgiveness*, unless he be identical with the Servant whose mission it is to 'justify' many by bearing their iniquities? The whole thrust of Isaiah 53 was summed up in Jesus' own words to his disciples when he emphasized that 'the Son of Man came not to be served but to serve, and to give his life as a ransom for many' (Mark 10:45).

These words are a summary of Isaiah 53 (except that Jesus substitutes 'Son of Man' for 'Servant of the Lord'), not a quotation from it. The one occasion when he is said to have explicitly quoted words from Isaiah 53 is recorded in Luke 22:37, where he tells his disciples at the Last Supper 'that this scripture must be fulfilled in me, "And he was reckoned with the transgressors" (Isaiah 53:12); for what is written about me has its fulfilment.' But here he means that henceforth his companions will be treated as outlaws; he is not referring directly to his own sacrifice.

The Servant's witnesses

In the gospel of John it is possible that John the Baptist's proclamation of 'the lamb of God, who takes away the sin of the world' (John 1:29) echoes the description of one who, suffering for the sins of others, remains silent 'like a lamb that is led to the slaughter' (Isaiah 53:7).

We have a more direct reference in Acts 3:13, where Peter begins his address to the crowd in the temple court with the announcement that God has glorified his servant Jesus, disowned and done to death by men – an announcement which echoes the divine declaration at the outset of the fourth Servant

Song: 'Behold my servant ... shall be exalted and lifted up, and shall be very high.' (Isaiah 52:13.) Later in the book of Acts comes the story of the Ethiopian treasurer, who was beguiling his homeward journey by reading the book of Isaiah in his chariot, and was accosted by Philip the evangelist as he read aloud some sentences from Isaiah 53. 'Do you understand what you are reading?' Philip asked. 'How can I,' replied the Ethiopian, 'unless someone guides me?' He invited Philip to come up into the chariot with him and tell him who the prophet was speaking about, whereupon Philip 'began with this scripture and told him the good news of Jesus' (Acts 8:27–35).

Paul does not make much direct reference to the Servant Songs, but it has been suggested above (page 57) that Isaiah 53 was one of the passages in his mind when he said that Christ's death and resurrection took place 'in accordance with the scriptures' (1 Corinthians 15:3–4). In Philippians 2:5–11 he reproduces what some people think to have been a very early Christian hymn about one who 'was in the form of God' but humbled himself to become man and humbled himself yet farther to suffer 'the death of the cross', who was then 'highly exalted' by God and given the name and status of universal supremacy. The outline is that of the fourth Servant Song, and when Christ is said to have 'emptied himself ... unto death' we have a virtual translation of the statement that the Servant 'poured out his soul to death' (Isaiah 53:12). Another echo of Isaiah 53 has been discerned in Romans 4:25, where Christ is said to have been 'delivered up for our trespasses'.

The letter to the Hebrews borrows at least one phrase from Isaiah 53 – from the last verse – when it says that Christ 'was offered once for all to bear the sins of many' (Hebrews 9:28).

But it is in 1 Peter that the most wholesale use is made of Isaiah 53 when the readers, who are being prepared for the outbreak of persecution, are reminded of the example of Christ (1 Peter 2:22–25):

He committed no sin; no guile was found on his lips. When he

was reviled, he did not revile in return; when he suffered, he did
not threaten; but he trusted to him who judges justly. He himself
bore our sins in his body on the tree, that we might die to sin
and live to righteousness. By his wounds you have been healed.
For you were straying like sheep, but have now returned to the
Shepherd and Guardian of you souls.

Let these words be compared with Isaiah 53:5–12 and it will
be realized that they present a selection, with Christian commentary, of salient phrases from those verses.

The righteous sufferer

Another figure in the Old Testament who has made his contribution to the New Testament presentation of Christ and his
work is the righteous sufferer whom we meet especially in the
Psalms. The righteous sufferer is not a single individual; he
is often the psalmist himself, but the language in which he pours
out his soul to God lent itself not only to the early Christians
when they spoke of Christ but to Christ himself. The righteous
sufferer complains of the treachery of a false friend: 'even my
bosom friend in whom I trusted, who ate of my bread, has
lifted his heel against me.' (Psalm 41:9.) According to John
13:18, these very words were quoted by Jesus at the Last Supper
when he revealed the presence of a traitor at the table.

Above all, in the bitterest hour of anguish and desolation
on the cross, Jesus made his own the outcry of another righteous
sufferer: 'My God, my God, why hast thou forsaken me?'
(Mark 15:34). Indeed, Psalm 22, which opens with these words,
provides some of the language which is woven into the passion
narrative (verses 8, 16, 18):

'He committed his cause to the LORD; let him deliver him,
   let him rescue him, for he delights in him!' ...
   they have pierced my hands and my feet ...
they divide my garments among them,
   and for my raiment they cast lots.

In the second part of the psalm the cry for help is answered and passes into an outburst of praise: this too is applied to Christ, as when verse 22 is put into his mouth in Hebrews 2:12:

> I will proclaim thy name to my brethren,
>> in the midst of the congregation I will praise thee.

Another psalm in which the prayer of a righteous suffer makes its contribution to the passion narrative is Psalm 69. We read, for example, in Matthew 27:34 that, when Jesus was about to be crucified, 'they offered him wine to drink, mingled with gall'; and no one who is acquainted with the Old Testament can miss the reference to Psalm 69:21 –

> they gave me gall for my food,
>> and for my thirst they gave me vinegar to drink.

This psalm, indeed, was drawn upon in the most various ways by the New Testament writers as they bore their witness to Christ. The first half of verse 9, for instance, is quoted by John the evangelist when he describes Christ's cleansing of the temple: 'His disciples remembered that it was written, "Zeal for thy house will consume me."' (John 2:17.) And the second half of the same verse is quoted by Paul in a completely different setting when he urges his readers to show consideration to others rather than to please themselves: 'For Christ did not please himself; but, as it is written, "The reproaches of those who reproached thee fell on me."' (Romans 15:3.)

As Peter said when preaching Christ in the house of Cornelius: 'To him' – to his work as well to his person – 'all the prophets bear witness' (Acts 10:43).

10

THE FUTURE WORK
OF CHRIST:
ACCORDING TO JOHN

Two 'greater works'

On the occasion when Jesus scandalized his hearers in Jerusalem
by claiming that he was entitled to keep on working, even on
the sabbath day, because his Father kept on working (see
page 28), he went on to say that, as the Son, he did whatever
the Father did. Perhaps he drew an object-lesson from his boy-
hood memories of the carpenter's workshop in Nazareth. He
had watched Joseph doing his work there and imitated him,
thus serving his unofficial apprenticeship in preparation for the
day when he himself would in his turn become the carpenter
of Nazareth.

That early experience may have been a kind of parable of
his relationship with his heavenly Father. 'The Father loves
the Son,' he said, 'and shows him all that he himself is doing.'
(John 5:20.) The religious authorities in Jerusalem had been
shocked by what Jesus had already done, but, relatively speaking, they hadn't seen anything yet. Jesus went on to say that
his Father would show him even greater works than had been
shown so far, and when Jesus performed these greater works,
there would be real ground for amazement.

What were these greater works which were yet to be done?
They were, more particularly, two works which were pre-
eminently the prerogative of God – the raising of the dead, and
the pronouncement of final judgement.

The work of judgement

When Jesus claimed that the Father conferred on him the right to raise the dead and judge them, he must have seemed to pass beyond the limits of daring. Here are his words, as John reports them: 'As the Father raises the dead and gives them life, so also the Son gives life to whom he will. The Father judges no one, but has given all judgment to the Son, that all may honour the Son, even as they honour the Father.' (John 5:21–23.)

Is it conceivable that Jesus could have spoken such words as these? Since our concern is with what the Bible teaches about the work of Christ, and the gospel of John is part of the Bible, we are surely bound to treat them seriously. And John's account does not go impossibly farther than what the other gospels say. According to our earliest gospel, Jesus told his disciples that if any one was ashamed of him or his teaching in the generation of his ministry, 'of him will the Son of Man also be ashamed, when he comes in the glory of his Father with the holy angels' (Mark 8:38). This appears to ascribe a judicial function to the Son of Man, and indeed Matthew makes that quite explicit in his version of the same saying: 'the Son of Man is to come with his angels in the glory of his Father, and then he will repay everyone for what he has done.' (Matthew 16:27.)

If the Son of Man is identical with Jesus himself, then Christians have good authority for addressing their Lord in the words of an ancient hymn: 'We believe that thou shalt come to be our judge.' In the record of John at which we have been looking, Jesus is not only identified with the Son of Man: the fact that he is the Son of Man is the ground for his exercising judgement. 'As the Father has life in himself, so he has granted the Son also to have life in himself, and *has given him authority to execute judgment, because he is the Son of Man.*' (John 5:26–27.)

But why 'because he is the Son of Man'? Why not 'because he is the Son of God'? Because, once more, behind this New Testament passage lies Daniel's vision of the day of judgement in which 'one like a son of man' receives universal sovereignty from God. In Old and New Testament times sovereignty always carried with it the right to administer judgement (as indeed it still does). Of the Messiah of David's line the prophet says (Isaiah 11:3-4):

> He shall not judge by what his eyes see,
>   or decide by what his ears hear;
> but with righteousness he shall judge the poor,
>   and decide with equity for the meek of the earth.

Similarly when the Servant of the Lord is introduced at the beginning of Isaiah 42, it is said of him:

> He will bring forth justice to the nations...;
>   he will faithfully bring forth justice.
> He will not fail or be discouraged'
>   till he has established justice in the earth;
>   and the coastlands wait for his law.

So in the setting of Daniel 7, where 'one like a son of man' receives sovereignty,

> the court sat in judgment,
>   and the books were opened.

The sovereignty bestowed on 'one like a son of man' is judicial as well as royal, and it is because Jesus is identified with *that* Son of Man that, according to John 5:27, he has been given 'authority to execute judgment'.

The raising of the dead

The passing of final judgement was closely associated in Jewish belief with the raising of the dead. For the raising of the dead as well as for the judgement of the end-time authority could be found in the book of Daniel: 'many of those who sleep in the dust of the earth shall awake' (Daniel 12:2). True, their awakening is not ascribed to the activity of the Son of Man in Daniel 12 as the raising of the dead is in John 5:21; but resurrection and judgement went closely together.

Now Jesus did not deny the current expectation: he endorsed

it. Daniel foretold a twofold division on the day of resurrection: 'some to everlasting life, and some to shame and everlasting contempt' (Daniel 12:2). This is echoed quite clearly in John 5:28–29, immediately after the mention of the Son of Man:

> Do not marvel at this; for the hour is coming when all who are in the tombs will hear his voice and come forth, those who have done good, to the resurrection of life, and those who have done evil, to the resurrection of judgement [i.e. adverse judgement, condemnation].

Eternal life now

But these are not the most important words about resurrection and judgement in Jesus' discourse recorded in John 5. Both resurrection and judgement in the future sense are simply the signature or seal affixed to a process going on in the present. Here and now, according to Jesus' words in John 5:24, 'he who hears my word and believes him who sent me, has eternal life; he does not come into judgment [condemnation], but has passed from death to life.' 'Eternal life' is another way of saying 'the life of the age to come' – that is, resurrection life. So, the person who believes in Jesus has resurrection life here and now. This is repeated several times throughout the gospel. If 'the hour is coming when all who are in the tombs will hear his voice and come forth', it is also affirmed that 'the hour is coming, *and now is*, when the dead will hear the voice of the Son of God, and those who hear will live' (John 5:25). It is happening already wherever the gospel is heard:

> He speaks and, listening to his voice,
> New life the dead receive.

The same teaching is found in the story of the raising of Lazarus in John 11. Lazarus was dead and buried by the time Jesus arrived at Bethany; and when Martha, one of the dead man's sisters, went to meet Jesus, he comforted her with the assurance, 'Your brother will rise again.' She took this to be a conventional condolence and said, 'Yes, I know; he will rise again in the resurrection at the last day.' Jesus did not contradict her; he himself believed and taught that the dead would rise 'at the last day'. But he told her something that she did not know before: 'I am the resurrection and the life. He who believes in me, though he die, yet shall he live, and whoever lives and believes in me shall never die.' (John 11:23–26.)

These words are frequently, and fittingly, repeated at Christian funeral services. But what do they mean? Those who believe in Jesus, the ever-living one, are so closely united to him by faith that they share his life. His life is nothing less than the life of God, residing in him (because he has 'life in himself') and communicated to his people. Those who receive this life from him receive a life which can never be terminated by death: 'whoever lives and believes in me shall never die.' If such a person experiences bodily death, his essential being cannot die but goes on living: 'though he die, yet shall he live.' No wonder another New Testament writer (Paul) speaks concisely of 'Christ our life' (Colossians 3:4).

So, when at the last day 'those who have done good' come forth 'to the resurrection of life', that will but confirm and ratify what is already true of them. Jesus' promise to his disciples, 'Because I live, you will live also,' (John 14:19) will be consummated on the resurrection day, but it begins to be fulfilled in their experience the moment they first become his disciples.

Present self-judgement

And what of the other company that comes forth on the last day – 'those who have done evil, to the resurrection of judgment'? Here too it is no arbitrary sentence that is passed. The judgement pronounced then is the judgement which they have already passed on themselves.

Towards the end of Jesus' public ministry in Jerusalem John presents him as saying, 'I did not come to judge the world but to save the world' (John 12:47). What this means is spelt out more fully by the same evangelist at an earlier stage in his gospel (John 3:17–19):

> God did not send the Son into the world to judge [condemn] the world, but that the world might be saved through him. He who believes in him is not condemned; he who does not believe is condemned already, because he has not believed in the name of the only Son of God. And this is the judgment [condemnation], that the light has come into the world, and men loved darkness rather than light, because their deeds were evil.

Jesus, by his own account, did not come to judge, but his presence and ministry set up a process of self-judgement wherever he went. Therefore we find him saying, in words which at first sight contradict those already quoted, 'For judgment I came into this world,' (John 9:39). But what he meant was this: judgement implies decision and discrimination. In every place to which he came there were those who believed in him and accepted his teaching, and there were those who ignored or rejected both him and his teaching. Thus, as John puts it more than once, 'there was a division among the people over him' (John 7:43; 10:19).

But by their response to him, men and women passed judgement on themselves – for life or for condemnation. One of the figures under which Jesus is described in the gospel of John is 'the light of the world'. When the light shone into the surrounding darkness, some were attracted to it; others avoided it, and by avoiding it showed themselves in their true character. Those who have adverse judgement pronounced against them at the last day are those who have been 'condemned already' – and self-condemned at that – in this present life.

Response to the truth

The earliest Christian preaching emphasized that Jesus was the one 'ordained by God to be judge of the living and the dead' (Acts 10:42). Sometimes this is presented in pictorial terms, as in the parable of the sheep and the goats (Matthew 25:31–46), or the vision of the great white throne (Revelation 20:11–15). Here we have concentrated on the teaching in the gospel of John. John wrote for people who did not have the background which made these pictorial terms easy to understand – he wrote, indeed, for people like ourselves, at a distance in time and place from the circumstances of Jesus' ministry. But he wrote in such a way as to bring out the permanent and universal meaning of all that Jesus did and taught. And, regarding the subjects which we have been considering in the last few pages, the lesson is this: whether for eternal life or for eternal judgement, now is the hour of decision. We make the decision ourselves, by our response to Christ. And if we ask a question which John does not ask – what about the millions who have never been personally confronted by Christ and his claims? – we may discover that John points to the answer. The Christ of whom he writes is the incarnation of the eternal Word of God, the embodiment of eternal truth. Even those who have never been personally confronted by Christ and his claims are confronted at times by what they recognize to be the truth – and they may accept it or refuse it. 'For this I was born,' said Jesus to Pilate, 'and for this I have come into the world, to bear witness to the truth. Every one who is on the side of truth heeds my voice.' (John 18:37.)

The one who is ordained by God to be the judge of the living and the dead is the one who is himself the truth as well as the light. 'He who does what is true comes to the light,' says John (John 3:21), and when such a person comes forth at his life-giving call on the last day, it will be to greet the judge as one who is at the same time redeemer and friend.

11

THE FUTURE WORK OF CHRIST: ACCORDING TO PAUL

An examination of John's teaching only might appear to be one-sided, so we go to another biblical writer who also says some things of great importance about what Christ is going to do.

First fruits and harvest

We have referred more than once to Paul's insistence in 1 Corinthians 15:3–4, that the death and resurrection of Christ took place 'in accordance with the scriptures' (see pages 57, 111). In this chapter Paul is particularly concerned with the resurrection of Christ. He emphasizes not only that it was foretold in the Old Testament scriptures but also that its historical actuality is confirmed by the many independent witnesses to whom the risen Christ appeared. He emphasizes this, not because his readers were entertaining doubts about the resurrection of Christ but because some of them were entertaining doubts about the resurrection of Christians. He insists that the resurrection of Christ and the resurrection of his people are so closely and logically interwoven that to deny the latter is to deny the former; contrariwise, to affirm the former is to affirm the latter.

In ancient Israel the first ripe sheaves of barley or wheat were dedicated to God as an acknowledgement that the whole harvest was his good gift. The first ripe sheaves, the first fruits,

were a sign of the plentiful harvest soon to be reaped. Paul
uses this as an object-lesson: the resurrection of Christ is the
presentation of the first fruits, and the resurrection of his
people is the following harvest. Between these two resurrections,
he says, Christ is reigning until all his enemies have been
subdued.

Among those enemies, those hostile 'principalities and
powers' at which we have looked in chapter 5, there is one
that is specially intractable and takes longer to put down than
any of the others. That one is death, 'the last enemy'. But at
the end even death will die from the mortal stroke it received
in the death of Christ. The death of death – in other words,
the coming resurrection – marks the completion of Christ's
present reign and coincides with his appearance in glory.

Resurrection and judgement

Paul tends to speak of *God* as raising the dead and of *God*
as executing final judgement, but makes it plain that he
accomplishes both these activities through Christ. 'Since we
believe that Jesus died and rose again, even so, *through Jesus*,
God will bring with him those who have fallen asleep.'
(1 Thessalonians 4:14.) Indeed, he goes on in that same passage
to ascribe the rising of 'the dead in Christ' to the 'cry of
command' heard (along with the archangel's voice and the
trumpet of God) when 'the Lord himself [i.e. Christ] will
descend from heaven' (1 Thessalonians 4:16). So, as James
Montgomery paraphrases Paul's words:

> The Lord himself shall come,
> And shout the quickening word.

So far as judgement is concerned, Paul speaks of 'that day when,
according to my gospel, God will judge people's hidden secrets
through Christ Jesus' (Romans 2:16). Elsewhere he speaks
indiscriminately of 'the judgment seat of God' (Romans 14:10)
or 'the judgment seat of Christ' (2 Corinthians 5:10), before
which we must all appear. Christ, then, is the agent of God

in resurrection and judgement for Paul as much as for John.

To go back to 1 Corinthians 15, Paul adds something there to what he had taught before. He repeats what he had said earlier – in 1 Thessalonians 4:16, for example – that at the return of Christ his people who have died will be raised again, brought back to life by God 'with him' (that is, as Christ himself was brought back to life). In 1 Corinthians 15:44 he makes it plain that the body that is raised belongs to a different order from the present mortal body. This is a 'natural' or 'physical' body; the resurrection body is a 'spiritual' body. Elsewhere he speaks of the resurrection body as being of the same order as Christ's resurrection body: the Saviour for whom we wait 'will change our lowly body to be like his glorious body' (Philippians 3:21). 'As we have borne the image of the man of dust [Adam], we shall also bear the image of the man of heaven.' (1 Corinthians 15:49.) Our present bodies are the means by which we communicate with our present earthly environment: something of a different order will be necessary for communicating with the new environment of the resurrection life.

But what of those who are still alive on earth when the momentous event takes place? How can they, in mortal bodies of flesh and blood, participate in the new order which will then be introduced? Briefly, they cannot. They too will have to undergo a change, and this is the new teaching that Paul adds. He himself had learned it by a revelation from God; that is what he means by saying, 'Lo! I tell you a mystery.' (1 Corinthians 15:51.) A 'mystery' in the New Testament is usually some form of truth formerly unknown but now for the first time divulged; and that is what the word means here. When the dead are raised, says Paul, living believers will be transformed simultaneously – 'in a moment, in the twinkling of an eye' (1 Corinthians 15:52). For both groups mortality must be displaced by immortality.

Christ will then have fulfilled the work which he is doing from his present state of enthronement, just as on the cross he fulfilled the work which he had to do on earth. Therefore he hands back his present royal power to God, who invested

him with it. This does not mean any reduction in status for
Christ; it means that the kingdom of Christ is now merged in
the eternal kingdom of God. Thus Christ continues to 'reign
for ever and ever'. God will then be 'all in all' (1 Corinthians
15:28). Thanks to the work of Christ, that is to say, God will
be universally acknowledged and obeyed, in all his goodness
and love.

Paul makes it plain that all, good and bad alike, will be judged
by God through Christ. He himself always kept in view the
day when he would have to render an account of his life and
service: 'It is the Lord who judges me.' (1 Corinthians 4:4.)
But he has little to say about resurrection for the wicked.
According to Acts 24:15 he declared before the Roman governor
of Judaea that he believed in 'a resurrection of both the just
and the unjust'. But in his letters he is silent about the resurrection of the 'unjust'. If in 1 Corinthians 15:22 he says that 'as
in Adam all die, so also in Christ shall all be made alive', the
next verse shows what is meant by the phrase 'in Christ': the
reference is to 'those who belong to Christ'.

Resurrection life now

As John speaks of resurrection in both a present and a future
aspect, so does Paul. Those who believe in Christ are united
with him, so closely that his death is reckoned theirs, and his
resurrection also is reckoned theirs. This is the significance that
Paul attaches to baptism: it is the sacrament of union with him
who died and rose again, 'so that as Christ was raised from
the dead by the glory of the Father, we too might walk in newness
of life' (Romans 6:4). Here and now, that is to say, those who
believe in Christ receive a share in the power of his risen life
and so are enabled (by the Spirit of Christ within them) to die
to sin and live to righteousness. Paul's own present ambition
was to know Christ 'and the power of his resurrection' (Philippians 3:10). If that involved him in 'the fellowship of his sufferings' – the sufferings which he endured for Christ's sake in
the course of his apostolic ministry – then God be thanked:

that also would help to fulfil his ambition to know Christ. To know Christ properly meant to share his sufferings as well as his resurrection life.

After death, what?

In all his earlier references to the resurrection of the people of Christ at his advent, Paul has nothing to say about a matter which one would have expected to be of considerable personal interest. He comforts those whose Christian friends have died with the assurance that they will be brought back from death at the advent of Christ, but he says nothing of their condition of existence between death and resurrection. He seems for a good part of his Christian life to have reckoned with the probability that he himself would still be alive when the advent took place. Of course he did not know when it would take place: 'of that day or that hour,' said Jesus, 'no one knows' (Mark 13:32). But as time went on, it became increasingly probable (not to say a near-certainty) that he himself would die first. In that case he would share in the resurrection of 'those who belong to Christ' when Christ came.

But now the question of what happens between death and resurrection became one of acute concern to himself. For Paul, the thought of being disembodied for any length of time – divested of the physical body and not yet invested with the resurrection body – was intolerable; it would mean spiritual nakedness and isolation. He faces this problem in 2 Corinthians 5:1–10, where he expresses the confidence that investiture will not be postponed: 'we know that if the earthly tent we live in is taken down, we have a building from God, a house not made with hands, eternal in the heavens.' The new 'housing' or 'embodiment' is ready, waiting to be put on. It is impossible that anyone who knows what it means to be 'in Christ' in this present life will be separated from him after this life ends. On the contrary, to be 'away from the body' will mean to be 'at home with the Lord' – instantaneously. Or, as Paul puts it later, in Philippians 1:21, 23, 'to me to live is Christ, and to die is gain. . . . My desire is to depart and be with Christ, for that is far better.' He plainly expects no conscious hiatus in the continued enjoyment of fellowship with Christ – not for one split second.

A wider perspective

In all this we have been thinking of the future work of Christ as it affects individual believers. But Paul's perspective is not confined to individuals, nor even to the believing community, the church. At the return of Christ in glory, the believing community will be glorified with him: 'when Christ our life appears,' the Colossians are told, 'then you also will appear with him in glory.' (Colossians 3:4.) But it is not just for their own sakes that they will be glorified.

There is a remarkable statement in Ephesians about God's ultimate purpose for the world. That purpose was conceived 'in Christ' from all eternity, to be manifested in living reality in God's good time, that all things – 'things in heaven and things on earth' – should be united in Christ. The New English Bible puts it like this (Ephesians 1:9–10):

> He has made known to us his hidden purpose – such was his will and pleasure determined beforehand in Christ – to be put into effect when the time was ripe: namely, that the universe, all in heaven and on earth, might be brought into a unity in Christ.

It was 'in Christ' that the plan was drawn before the world's creation; it is 'in Christ' that it is to be fulfilled. Then God will indeed be 'all in all'.

In the accomplishment of this plan the believing community has a crucial part to play. The church is the fellowship of those who have already been 'brought into a unity in Christ', reconciled through Christ to God and therefore reconciled one to another. The church is God's masterpiece of reconciling grace, an object-lesson of his wisdom 'to the principalities and powers in the heavenly places' (Ephesians 3:10). How far the church as it really is corresponds to this ideal picture is something which God can decide better than we can. But, according to Ephesians, the church is God's pilot scheme, so to speak, for the reconciled universe which he plans to bring about, and the instrument by which he will bring it about. The consummation of this plan depends on the work of Christ. At the cross 'God was in Christ reconciling the world to himself' (2 Corinthians 5:19). The first stage in this reconciling work has been the reconciliation of the believing community. When the time comes for the final stage, it will still be 'in Christ', through his reconciled people, that God reconciles the world to himself. The realization of God's eternal purpose hangs upon the reconciling death of Christ.

This realization of the eternal purpose is affirmed by Paul in a vivid paragraph in Romans 8. There he speaks of the resurrection of believers as our 'adoption as sons, the redemption of our bodies' (Romans 8:23). Believers are sons and daughters of God already, but the 'adoption' of which Paul speaks here is their public investiture as such. The body as well as the soul is the object of Christ's redeeming work. That is why Paul insists to the Corinthians that bodily actions are not morally irrelevant. Even this present mortal body is 'a temple of the Holy Spirit'; therefore, he says, 'glorify God in your body' (1 Corinthians 6:19–20). And that the Lord claims the body as his own will be shown on the day when it is transformed into the likeness of his glorious body.

But it is not only those who are to be manifested with their Lord in glory who look forward to that day. All creation looks forward to it. In the story of the fall in Genesis 3 the earth and its produce shared in the curse incurred by man's first disobedience; so, Paul implies, the removal of that curse by the work of Christ means blessing even for the inanimate creation. 'For the creation waits with eager longing for the revealing of the sons of God.' Why? Because creation was subjected involuntarily to change and decay, to frustration and futility. Perhaps Paul has in mind the refrain of Ecclesiastes: 'Vanity of vanities, all is vanity.' But this state of affairs is not to last for ever: the work of Christ provides sure hope that 'the creation itself will be set free from its bondage to decay and obtain the glorious liberty of the children of God' (Romans 8:19–21). The strains and stresses which beset creation now are the birth-pangs of the new order.

With the recent revival of concern for our physical environment and for 'ecology' we may find it easier to grasp part of Paul's thought here, although he places the whole matter in the context of the purpose of God and the work of Christ. The environment does indeed depend very largely, for better for worse, on human conduct. Selfish exploitation (an integral element of the fall) can turn the good earth into a dustbowl; responsible stewardship (part of the creation 'mandate' to the human family) can make the desert blossom as the rose. When, then, the entail of the fall is finally abolished by the work of Christ, who is the 'last Adam', the effect on creation must be beneficial. In the resurrection order, Paul envisages new men and women clothed in 'spiritual bodies'; how does he envisage the renovated creation? Probably he has in mind the prophet's vision of 'new heavens and a new earth' which God will bring into being in the age of restoration (Isaiah 65:17; 66:22), but he does not go into details. He does, however, leave his readers in no doubt that the renewal of creation, as well as the final and complete redemption of the children of God, is the effect of the saving work of Christ.

12

THE SAVING WORK OF CHRIST

Unity in diversity

We have considered the various ways in which the New Testament writers (and some Old Testament writers too) set forth the work of Christ. Is there sufficient agreement among them for us to sum up the main lines of their teaching in a few comprehensive statements? I believe there is.

Christ our salvation

For example, all of them, in one form or another, bear witness to the *saving* effect of the work of Christ. Some of them give him the title 'Saviour'; nearly all of them – in so far as they touch on his work at all – say that he has accomplished our salvation. 'Salvation' in the ears of many people has an old-fashioned or technical sound. We are familiar with it as part of the name of the Salvation Army, and some of us hear it in church; but it does not belong to the current coin of everyday speech. Even so, we are always glad to learn, when a plane has crashed, that most of those on board were 'saved'; we know at once what the verb means in that setting and 'salvation' is the corresponding noun. Think of other words which in some degree share the same meaning as 'salvation': deliverance, security, liberation, victory.

People want deliverance or security from danger or trouble, liberation from bondage or oppression, victory over enemies.

When the father of John the Baptist sang a hymn of praise to
God for the birth of his son, he thanked God for fulfilling the
ancient promises 'that we should be saved from our enemies,
and from the hand of all that hate us' (Luke 1:71). In a different
setting this could have meant the national liberation of the
people of Israel from the Roman power which dominated their
land. But as we read on in the gospel of Luke, it is plain that
this is not the kind of salvation envisaged – either there or
anywhere else in the New Testament. In the next chapter of
the same gospel Simeon of Jerusalem takes the infant Jesus in
his arms and thanks God that he has lived to behold this day
(Luke 2:30–32):

> for mine eyes have seen thy salvation
> which thou hast prepared in the presence of all peoples,
> a light for revelation to the Gentiles,
> and for glory to thy people Israel.

Here Christ himself is greeted as the very embodiment of
God's salvation – not for one favoured nation only, but for all
nations. It is not deliverance from imperial oppression that is
in view here. In Simeon's words, indeed, we have an echo of
words addressed by God to his Servant in Isaiah 49:6 –

> It is too light a thing that you should be my servant
>   to raise up the tribes of Jacob
>   and to restore the survivors of Israel;
> I will give you as a light to the nations,
>   that my salvation may reach to the end of the earth.

What was said of the Servant by the prophet has come true
in Christ. He has come, and 'now is the acceptable time; . . . now
is the day of salvation.' (2 Corinthians 6:2,) That is Paul speaking, not Luke, but he speaks to the same effect; indeed, Paul
himself is quoting Isaiah 49:8, from the same Servant song as
the one which Simeon echoes. Luke reports Peter as bearing
public witness to Jesus and saying that 'there is salvation in
no one else, for there is no other name under heaven given among
men by which we must be saved' (Acts 4:12). John says in his

gospel that Jesus came into the world 'that the world might be saved through him' (John 3:17).

But saved from what? According to Matthew, he was to be called Jesus (which in Hebrew contains the word for 'salvation') because 'he will save his people *from their sins*' (Matthew 1:21). And Zechariah, John the Baptist's father, who speaks of being 'saved from our enemies', goes on to say (Luke 1:76–77) that his son's mission will be

to go before the Lord to prepare his ways,
to give knowledge of salvation to his people
in the forgiveness of their sins.

'Every one who believes in him,' said Peter as he preached Christ to a Gentile audience for the first time, 'receives forgiveness of sins through his name.' (Acts 10:43.) The readers of Peter's first letter are told: 'As the outcome of your faith you receive the salvation of your souls.' (1 Peter 1:9.) The readers of John's first letter are told: 'your sins are forgiven for his sake.' (1 John 2:12.) And the opening doxology of the book of Revelation ascribes eternal glory and dominion 'to him who loves us and has freed us from our sins by his blood' (Revelation 1:5).

The means of salvation

We have drawn these statements from a fairly wide variety of New Testament writers to show their general agreement that the salvation which Christ has accomplished includes as one of its major features the forgiveness of sins and that it is received by faith – personal faith in Christ. Each writer has an emphasis and perspective of his own, but on the main character of the work of Christ they are at one. Not only so; the last text quoted says that Christ has set his people free from their sins 'by his blood' – that is, simply, by his death or, more precisely, by his sacrificial death. We have seen how Jesus himself said that he came 'to give his life as a ransom for many' (Mark 10:45). We have seen how Paul gives the first principle of the gospel preached by himself and other apostles as 'Christ died for our sins' (1 Corinthians 15:3). We have seen how the writer to the Hebrews says that Christ 'appeared once for all . . . to put away sin by the sacrifice of himself' (Hebrews 9:26). We have seen how Peter's first letter tells how Christ 'himself bore our sins in his body on the tree' (1 Peter 2:24).

Indeed, the only major New Testament writer who does not explicitly ascribe saving power to the *death* of Christ is Luke. He does, however, repeatedly insist that forgiveness of sins is received through Christ, and through no other. How, then (we may ask), apart from his death and resurrection, does Christ make forgiveness available to those who believe in him?

Advocacy and expiation

One further text which will repay consideration comes in John's first letter. Believers in Christ, says John, should not sin; 'but if any one does sin, we have an advocate with the Father, Jesus Christ the righteous; and he is the expiation for our sins, and not for ours only but also for (the sins of) the whole world.' (1 John 2:1–2.)

Here Jesus' work for his people is described in two ways: he is their 'advocate with the Father' and he is the 'expiation' for their sins.

When John calls him our 'advocate', he means something quite similar to what the author of Hebrews has in mind when he calls him our 'high priest'. The term 'high priest' is borrowed from the language of the temple; the term 'advocate' is borrowed from the language of the law-court. Paul had employed the language of the law-court in Romans 8:33–34, which was quoted in chapter 5 (page 68). He does not actually use the term 'advocate' there, but he reproduces its meaning when he says that the risen Christ 'makes intercession' for his people before the throne of God, acting as their counsel for the defence. Anyone who wants a good commentary on John's description of Christ as our 'advocate with the Father' will find one in the full text of Charles Wesley's great hymn, the first verse of which runs:

Arise, my soul, arise,
　　Shake off thy guilty fears;
The bleeding sacrifice
　　In my behalf appears:
Before the throne my Surety stands;
My name is written on his hands.

But what of John's further statement, that Christ is 'the
expiation for our sins'? 'Expiation' is the word chosen by the
Revised Standard Version. The meaning of 'expiation' is
brought out fairly well by the Good News Bible: 'Christ himself
is the means by which our sins are forgiven.' Our sins need
to be forgiven: through him they are forgiven. That is at least
part of John's meaning. The New English Bible says, 'He is
himself the remedy for the defilement of our sins.' Our sins
pollute us; through him we are made clean. That also is part
of John's meaning. The translators of the New English Bible
were probably influenced by 1 John 1:7, which they render:

> if we walk in the light, as he [God] himself is in the light, then
> we share together a common life, and we are being cleansed from
> every sin by the blood of Jesus his Son.

The older English versions say that Christ 'is the propitiation
for our sins'. The word 'propitiation' is practically equivalent
to 'atonement'. The Living Bible in its footnote to 1 John 2:2
suggests the rendering 'atoning sacrifice'. But in its text it
paraphrases this by saying,

> He is the one who took God's wrath against our sins upon himself,
> and brought us into fellowship with God; and he is the forgiveness
> for our sins, and not only ours but all the world's.

By God's 'wrath' is meant the reaction of his holiness and
purity against sin and evil of every kind. There is a tendency
to avoid the use of this word in relation to God because 'wrath',
when it refers to a human emotion, commonly denotes anger
which has crossed the boundary which separates righteous
indignation from unbridled fury. It is sometimes replaced by
'retribution', as though to emphasize that in a moral universe

evil of one sort brings evil of another sort in its train. But it is not an impersonal force, for the moral universe is God's universe – the universe in which, as Jesus said, not a sparrow falls to the ground unnoticed by the heavenly Father. If retribution were an impersonal force, not much could be done about it, perhaps; but if it is the personal judgement of God, the situation is different. What the gospel declares is that God's free, sovereign, unconditioned grace has intervened and retrieved the situation. God in Christ has taken the judgement on himself. The operation of 'wrath' has thus been reversed or counteracted. Whichever word or phrase may be used – atonement, expiation or any other – the important thing to emphasize is that it is something which God has provided for us in Christ to remove all obstacles to the free flow of his grace to us. It does not imply that we do something to appease God, so that he lets us off. It does not imply that Christ consented to suffer in order to persuade God to love us. Such a travesty of the truth is a slander on the character of God: it was because God loved the human race that Christ, his Son, identified himself with it, shared its troubles, bore its sins and thus exhausted in himself the retribution that those sins had incurred. John makes it doubly plain later in the same letter (1 John 4:9–11):

> In this the love of God was made manifest among us, that God sent his only Son into the world, so that we might live through him. In this is love, not that we loved God but that he loved us and sent his Son to be the expiation for our sins. My dear friends, if God so loved us, we also ought to love one another.

'And not for ours only,' John adds when he speaks of Christ as the expiation of our sins, 'but also for the whole world.' (1 John 2:2.) He will not allow his readers to think of their salvation in too restricted terms. The atoning sacrifice that has availed to wipe out their sins is sufficient to do the same for all. Jesus is 'the general Saviour of mankind' as well as the particular and personal Saviour of each individual believer; he is 'the Lamb of God, who takes away the sin of the world' (John 1:29).

The cure of sin

In this last quotation the singular 'sin' is used, whereas in the texts quoted above from 1 John and elsewhere we have the plural 'sins'. Is there any distinction between the singular and plural?

Sins (in the plural) may be described, in general, as acts of disobedience to the will of God. Disobedience to his will, indeed, does not always take the form of *acts*; it may take the form of *failure to act*. The distinction has often been drawn between 'sins of commission' (doing what should not be done) and 'sins of omission' (not doing what should be done). The disobedience may be conscious or unconscious. There is such a thing as knowing what is right and deliberately refusing to do it, even deliberately doing what is wrong instead – sinning 'with a high hand' (as it is called in Numbers 15:30). The law of Moses treated this kind of sin much more severely than any other kind.

Commoner, perhaps, is that failure to do the will of God which comes from not knowing his will, or from unintentionally disobeying it. The law of Moses provided for the forgiveness of such 'unwitting' sins if an appropriate sacrifice were offered to make atonement or reparation for them.

But the real trouble does not lie in individual sinful actions (positive or negative); it lies deeper. The real trouble lies with the condition briefly referred to as *sin* (in the singular). This condition is pictured sometimes as a state of rebellion against God, sometimes as estrangement from him. In either case reconciliation to God is the cure for the condition. To rebels God extends an amnesty; to those who are estranged from him he holds out the promise of restoration. Hamlet complained that the time was 'out of joint', and bewailed his misfortune in having been 'born to set it right'. But in reality it was Hamlet that was 'out of joint' and needed to be set right. Something like this can be said of the human predicament. Our relationship with God is 'out of joint', and needs to be set right. That is why our relationships within the human family – person with person, race with race, class with class, sex with sex – are also too often 'out of joint' and need to be set right. This matter of 'setting right', this double reconciliation, is part of the work of Christ, or the work of God in Christ. 'While we were enemies,' says Paul, 'we were reconciled to God by the death of his Son,' (Romans 5:10). It was by his death, too, that reconciliation was made possible on the human level: with reference to two previously opposed groups it is said (Ephesians 2:14–16) that Christ

is our peace, who has made us both one, and has broken down the dividing wall of hostility, ... that he might ... reconcile us both to God in one body through the cross, thereby bringing the hostility to an end.

The death of Christ on the cross is by far his greatest work. Also, according to the New Testament, it is by far the greatest work of God. Through it he has inaugurated his new creation, a greater work than the material creation. This was well brought out by Isaac Watts in what one authoritative judge has called 'the greatest of all hymns on the atonement written since the reformation' – the hymn which begins:

> Nature with open volume stands,
>   To spread her Maker's praise abroad;
> And every labour of his hands
>   Shows something worthy of a God.
>
> But in the grace that rescued man,
>   His brightest form of glory shines;
> Here, on the cross, 'tis fairest drawn,
>   In precious blood, and crimson lines.
>
> Here his whole Name appears complete:
>   Nor wit can guess, nor reason prove,
> Which of the letters best is writ –
>   The power, the wisdom, or the love.

Salvation in three tenses

A story is told of the nineteenth-century English scholar Bishop

Westcott. When he was Regius Professor of Divinity in Cambridge, it is said, he was approached by a zealous undergraduate with the personal question, 'Are you saved?' 'Ah,' said Westcott, 'a very good question. But tell me: do you mean...?' – and then he mentioned three passive participles of the Greek verb 'to save', indicating that his answer would depend on which of the three the student had in mind. 'I know I *have been saved*,' he said (except that he used the Greek forms, which are here put in italics in English); 'I believe I *am being saved*; and I hope by the grace of God that I *shall be saved*.'

Salvation has a past, a present and future reference. What we have been considering so far has to do with its past reference. The sacrificial work of Christ on the cross – his 'finished work' – has already done much for those who believe in him. It has cleansed them from the defilement of sin; it has absolved them of the judgement due to sin; it has cancelled the debt of sin; it has won them pardon for the guilt of sin; it has reconciled them to God. All this and more is involved in the past reference of salvation. It has been made available by the love of God in Christ, and it can be received and enjoyed by faith.

If salvation in the past reference is bound up with the death of Christ, salvation in the present reference is bound up with his risen life. This is how Paul puts it: 'if while we were enemies we were reconciled to God by the death of his Son, much more, now that we are reconciled, shall we be saved by his life.' (Romans 5:10.) Christ's present work for his people – his 'intercession' – procures for them the power to overcome the opposition of all the hostile forces in the universe, to remain free from the tyranny and enticement of sin, to live as his representatives and witnesses in this world, to overcome the fear of death by the sure hope of eternal life. It is difficult, and indeed unnecessary, to draw a clear distinction between this present work of Christ and the ministry of the Holy Spirit, for it is the Spirit who makes effective in the people of Christ not only what Christ has done for them in the past but what he is doing for them now.

Christians are never encouraged to adopt the attitude: 'Pull up the ladder, Jack; I'm all right.' As the work of Christ in the past was for others, so his present work is for others; and his people are the agents through whom he does his work in the world. Christians, therefore, must be known and recognized as people who live for others; otherwise there is no way of telling that they are the followers of Christ. The church, it has been aptly said, is a society which exists for the benefit of its non-members. If there is a sense in which they are saved 'out of this world', it is in order that they may be sent back into this world to be the messengers of God's peace, the instruments of Christ's redeeming activity in the world. As they work for him, he works in them.

The new world

Christ is the founder of a new humanity, and his people are members of this new humanity – the new humanity which is destined to grow until at last it absorbs and supersedes the 'old humanity' of 'B.C.' character. This new humanity was described by some early Christian writers as a 'third race' – no longer Jewish, no longer Gentile, but embracing and transcending both. Those who belong to it will exhibit its qualities, the qualities which characterize the way of Christ – giving service instead of receiving it, bearing the cross instead of inflicting it, saving its life by losing it, expending itself in love.

Perhaps the full flowering of the new humanity lies far off in the distant future; Christians today may be still foundation-members, relatively speaking. We do not know. But the existence of this new humanity is not only a token that the work of Christ is still going on, but a promise that it will one day reach its fulfilment. James is a New Testament writer whom we have not quoted because he has so little to say about the work of Christ, but writing about God to his fellow Christians, he says a remarkable thing which deserves to be quoted in this connexion: 'Of his own will he brought us forth by the word of truth that we should be a kind of first fruits of his creatures.' (James 1:18.) In other words, the people of Christ have been created anew through faith in him so as to be the 'first fruits' of the new creation – that new heaven and earth of a coming day to which the prophets looked forward.

This, then, brings us to the future reference of our salvation. Paul, who insists that believers in Christ are already 'justified' in God's sight, repeatedly speaks of salvation as something which lies in the future. 'Salvation is nearer to us now,' he writes to the Romans, 'than when we first believed' (Romans 13:11), and again: 'God shows his love for us in that while we were yet sinners Christ died for us. Since, therefore, we are now justified by his blood, much more shall we be saved by him from the wrath' – the final judgement on all that is evil (Romans 5:8–9). In one of his earliest letters he speaks of Jesus as our deliverer 'from the wrath to come' (1 Thessalonians 1:10).

Jesus himself, speaking of the onset of the end-time troubles, encouraged his disciples with the words 'he who endures to the end will be saved' (Mark 13:13). We who live nearly 2,000 years later have naturally a longer perspective than those disciples could have had, but the same encouragement is available for us. By his present work Christ gives his people the grace to endure; his future work will bring them final salvation and victory.

Some writers are able to enter confidently into much greater detail about the future work of Christ than this book has attempted to do. It is natural that there should be even greater disagreement about the interpretation of the future than about the interpretation of the past. But for those who take the witness of the New Testament seriously one thing is certain: Christ has won the decisive victory, 'the kingdom of the world has become the kingdom of our Lord and of his Christ, and he shall reign for ever and ever.' (Revelation 11:15.) Christians therefore are not building castles in the air or whistling to keep their courage up when they sing:

> Jesus shall reign where'er the sun
> Doth his successive journeys run;
> His kingdom stretch from shore to shore,
> Till moons shall wax and wane no more.

This is the promise of the gospel: that love and peace will triumph.

The hope is certain; the time-table is less important than has often been supposed. In a sermon preached last century on the subject 'Waiting for Christ', John Henry Newman made the point that, whereas the course of time before the first coming of Christ ran straight towards that event, the course of time since then has not run straight towards his second coming, but alongside it. Had it run straight towards his second coming, it would have run into it in the first Christian generation. But as it is, the course of time will ultimately merge with the presence of Christ, yet in such a way that while it runs alongside, the presence of Christ is equally near in all succeeding generations; his coming is always 'at hand'.

Meanwhile Christ continues the work he began on earth; the time is coming when he will consummate that work. 'I am sure,' said Paul to his friends at Philippi, 'that he who began a good work in you will bring it to completion at the day of Jesus Christ.' (Philippians 1:6.) This assurance is ours today, and in this assurance the hope of the world is secure.

INDEX

Aaron 73, 78
Abraham 55, 74, 85
Acts of the Apostles 44–50, 110, 111
adoption 127
advocate 133
Agrippa 104
Amen, the 88
angel of the divine presence 101
apocalyptic 87
apostles 49
appearances of the risen Christ 42, 43, 44, 56
ark of the covenant 75, 80
arrest of Jesus 38
atonement 59, 76, 77, 133, 134
Atonement, Day of 74–77, 83, 84

baptism 99, 124
baptism of Jesus 14, 15, 16, 127
baptism with the Spirit 16, 45, 46
Barnabas 48
beast from the abyss 87
Beelzebul 23
beginning 95, 98
Bethany 31, 117
Bethesda 28
blasphemy 29, 40
body of Christ 46
bread of life 24
Bunyan, J. 68, 90

Caesar 34, 35, 41, 90

Caesarea 13
Caesarea Philippi 30
Caiaphas 39, 63
Canaan 99
Carey, W. 66
chief priests 31, 35, 39
church 45, 46, 126
city of God 85
Colossians, letter to 66, 67, 96, 98, 99
commandments, ten 27, 34
Corinth 56
Corinthians, letters to 97, 98, 100, 121–25
Cornelius 13, 14, 113
covenant, new 36, 37, 83, 85
creation 88
creation, Christ in 94–99
creation, new 136, 138
cross, crucifixion 25, 26, 38, 41, 52, 54, 86, 98, 113, 127, 136
Cullmann, O. 65
curse of the law 52–55
curse, removal of 127

Damascus road 44, 52, 53, 56, 96
Daniel, book of 106, 110, 115, 116, 117
David 15, 74, 89, 116
D-day and V-day 65
Dead Sea Scrolls 62
death 64, 65, 122, 125, 126

death of Jesus 56, 57, 58, 131, 132, 136, 137
Dedication, Feast of 31
demonic forces 65–70
Deuteronomy, book of 100
dispersion 75
dragon 87

Egypt 36, 99, 100
Eleazar (son of Aaron) 78
Emmaus road 42, 43, 105
Ephesians, letter to 126
Ephesus 48
estrangement 135
eternal life 117, 118, 137
Ethiopian 111
evil, powers of 62–64
Exodus, book of 100, 101
expiation 131, 134

faith 54, 55, 60, 131
fall 127
Father (title of God) 13, 28, 114, 115
feeding of multitude 24, 29
forgiveness of sins 110, 131, 132

Gadarene demoniac 24
Galatians, letter to 62
Galilee 18, 19, 25, 28, 29, 30, 33, 35, 41, 104
Galilee, Lake of 23, 25, 29, 43
Gentiles 30, 32, 48, 51, 55
Gethsemane 38, 79
glory of God 99
grace 68, 69

Hallelujah chorus 91
Hanson, A. T. 93, 101
Hebrews, letter to 71–86, 96, 111, 132
Herod 20, 24, 29, 30, 33, 63
high priest (Jesus) 73, 74, 132
humanity, new 138
humanity of Jesus 79
hymns, early Christian 97, 111

Iconium 48
image of God 95, 96, 123
incarnation 94, 95, 120
intercession 69, 71, 132, 137
interpreter's house 90
Isaiah, book of 57, 90, 101, 104–12, 116
Israel 87

James, letter of 138
Jeremiah, book of 33, 83
Jerusalem 28, 29, 30, 31, 32, 36, 37, 39, 41, 47, 48, 72, 74, 75
Jewish Christians 72
Job 108
John the Baptist 14, 16, 19, 21, 29, 45, 46, 110, 130, 131
John, gospel of 45, 93, 94, 110, 115–19, 130
John, letters of 131, 132
John, Revelation to 87–93, 98, 131
Jordan 30
Joseph (carpenter) 114
Judaea 19, 31, 33
Judah (tribe) 73, 89
Judas the Galilean 19, 33
Judas Iscariot 35, 38
Jude, letter of 100, 101
judgement 16, 20, 53, 60, 92, 93, 114–19, 122, 134
justification 57, 58, 60, 61, 68, 139

king of the Jews 39
kingdom of God 14, 18, 19, 22, 23, 29, 30, 35, 91, 124

Lamb of God 77, 88, 89, 90, 101, 110, 134
Last Supper 36, 37
law 51–55, 58, 60, 83, 135
Lazarus (of Bethany) 31, 117
Levi (tribe) 73, 77
Leviticus, book of 74, 75
light 95, 96, 99, 119, 120

lion of tribe of Judah 89
Lord's Supper 99
Luke, gospel of 44, 130–32

Maccabees 59
manna 99
Mark, gospel of 34–41, 44, 115
martyrs 59
Masefield, J. 24
Matthew, gospel of 104, 105, 115, 131
Melchizedek 73, 74, 78
mercy seat 59, 75, 80
Messiah 13, 14, 15, 25, 26, 30, 40, 41, 52, 53, 56, 72, 74, 87, 89, 116
miracles 21, 22, 23, 27, 47, 48
Montgomery, J. 122
Moses 37, 73, 74, 78, 80, 83, 135
mystery 123

name of Jesus 47, 48
Nazareth 21, 105, 114
Nero 91
Numbers, book of 101

Old Testament 101, 102, 103–13
Olivet 33, 37

Pal, K. 66
Palestine 11
Passover, Feast of 31, 35, 36
Paul 43, 44, 46, 48, 49, 51–70, 71, 76, 100, 101, 104, 111, 121–28, 130, 131, 139
Pentecost, Feast of 43, 45
Peter 13, 14, 25, 26, 30, 43, 45, 46, 71, 84, 113, 130, 131, 132
Peter, letters of 104, 110, 111, 112
Pharaoh 99
Pharisees 29
Philip (evangelist) 111
Philip (tetrarch) 30
Philippians, letter to 111
Pierson, A. T. 49

Pilate 32, 34, 40, 41, 63, 120
pioneer 86
poor, the 20, 21
priesthood (of Christ) 71–85
principalities and powers 63, 64, 66–68, 96, 97, 122, 126
Priscilla 72
promised land 99
prophecy 103–13
propitiation 133
Proverbs, book of 97, 98
Psalms, book of 97, 112, 113
purpose, God's ultimate 126, 127

Qumran 62

raising of the dead 115–18
ransom 41, 131
rebellion 135
reconciliation 57, 58, 126, 127, 135–37
redemption 54, 58, 60, 127, 128
Red Sea (Sea of Reeds) 23, 99
resurrection (of Jesus) 42, 43, 44, 56, 64, 65, 121, 124, 125
resurrection (future) 64, 70, 117–18, 121, 122, 125, 127
retribution 133, 134
revealing of sons of God 127
Revelation – see John, Revelation to
righteous sufferer 112, 113
right hand of God 64, 73
Robinson, H. W. 109
rock 100, 101
Rome 19, 24, 29, 31–34, 38, 40, 43, 48, 49, 72, 88, 90
Romans, letter to 55, 58–60

sabbath 27, 28, 115
sacrifice 59, 74–86
salvation 129
Samaritans 48
Saviour 129
scapegoat 76

scroll of destiny 89
second coming 86, 125, 126, 140
self-judgement 118, 119
Servant of the Lord 15, 26, 57, 90, 106–12, 116, 130
Simeon 130
sin, sins 56, 57, 135
Sinai 80, 83
Son of God 15, 16, 17, 22, 40, 52, 73, 115, 116, 134
Son of Man 18, 25, 40, 41, 57, 105, 106, 110, 115
Spirit of God 13, 14, 15, 16, 18, 21, 23, 43, 45, 46, 49, 55, 63, 69, 104, 124, 127, 137
spiritual body 123, 128
spiritual sanctuary 79, 80, 85, 86
Stephen 40
synagogue 21, 27

tabernacle 74, 75, 80
Tabernacles, Feast of 31
taxes to Caesar 33, 34, 35
temple (at Jerusalem) 32, 33, 35, 39, 40, 47, 72, 74, 75, 113

temptation (testing) 16, 17, 24, 38, 79
Theophilus 44
Thessalonians, letters to 122
thorn in the flesh 69
trial of Jesus 39–41
truth 120

unity in diversity 129

victory of Christ 64–70, 96, 97

water of life 93
Watts, I. 77, 136
Wesley, C. 84, 132, 133
Westcott, B. F. 137
wilderness 17, 74, 76, 99–102
wisdom of God 63, 88, 97, 98, 99
Word (Logos) 92, 93, 120
wrath 133, 134

Zechariah (father of John the Baptist) 130, 131

FURTHER READING

Denney, J., *The Death of Christ* (Tyndale Press, 1951; reprinted from 1902 edition).

Forsyth, P. T., *The Work of Christ* (Collins/Fontana, 1965; reprinted from 1910 edition).

Green, E. M. B., *The Meaning of Salvation* (Hodder and Stoughton, 1965).

Hunter, A. M., *The Gospel Then and Now* (SCM Press, 1978).

Marshall, I. H., *The Work of Christ* (Paternoster Press, 1969).

Morris, L., *The Cross in the New Testament* (Paternoster Press, 1976; reprinted from 1965).

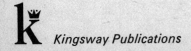

More than a carpenter

by Josh McDowell

What makes Jesus so different?

He may have been a good man, even a great teacher—but what has he got to do with our lives today?

Josh McDowell thought Christians must be out of their minds. He put them down. He argued against their faith. But then he discovered for himself the truth about Jesus, and experienced his life-changing power.

Here he brings answers for those who are as sceptical as he was—answers for those who have doubts about Jesus, his deity, his resurrection and his claim on their lives.

Over 900,000 copies now in print.

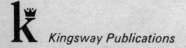

Kingsway Publications

My God is Real

by David Watson

If the things Christ said are not true, then the sooner we throw this Christianity into a funeral pyre the better....

On the other hand, if Christ's teaching is the truth, the position is very different. There may need to be radical changes in our lives, a new life altogether. What is necessary is that we should know what real Christianity is all about: and that is the purpose of this book.

A Falcon Book
Kingsway Publications

I Believe

by Colin Day

What do Christians believe?

This book is a guide to the basic beliefs of the Christian faith as expressed in the Apostles' Creed.

Far more than a simple list of doctrines, it explores the practical implications of our beliefs, challenging us to a greater depth of Christian commitment in our day-to-day living.

A Falcon Book
Kingsway Publications

Out of This World

Worldliness and the Christian

by John F. Balchin

'You are not of the world, but I chose you out of the world; therefore the world hates you' (John 15:19).

When God decided to make a people for himself, he could have removed them from the pressures of this world. But he didn't. Instead he called his people to a life that would glorify him right in the rough and tumble of everyday life and work. And he makes the same call today.

This book encourages Christians to live lives honouring to God in the midst of all that the twentieth century has to offer by way of false morality, materialism and a self-centred lifestyle. It challenges the church to avoid friendship with the world, while showing that Christians can remain involved in society as 'a colony of heaven on earth'.

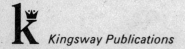

Kingsway Publications

Time to Share

by Jim Smith

Christians have a lot to share. But even the most well-meaning find it hard at times to witness to their faith lovingly and effectively.

Jim Smith has written for those who believe in 'doing evangelism' rather than just talking about it. With his feet on the ground and his sights set on the coming kingdom, he takes us through the steps of telling others the good news of Jesus Christ.

Here we see how to

- build friendships
- share the facts
- lead someone to the Lord
- support a new believer
- learn from mistakes
- silence the Enemy.

Through it all Jim encourages us with humour, realism and the thrill of being involved in the sovereign work of God.

A Falcon Book
Kingsway Publications